Wives Lives:
Tales from the Parsonage

Jill Anthony

Ruth Nesolk

WIVES LIVES:TALES FROM THE PARSONAGE

Jill Anthony & Faith Wesolik

46 Stories That
Inspire, Inform,
Support, and Entertain.

Outskirts Press, Inc.
Denver, Colorado

Outskirts Press, Inc.
http://www.outskirtspress.com

ISBN: 978-1-4327-2990-5

Library of Congress Control Number: 2009921978

Outskirts Press and the "OP" logo are trademarks belonging to Outskirts Press, Inc.

PRINTED IN THE UNITED STATES OF AMERICA

INTRODUCTION

Ministry can be a lonely profession for both the pastor and his wife. As ministers wives and as mothers, most of the child rearing and domestic activities (defined as anything that needs to be done) are often left to the minister's wife while her husband spends his days in counseling, running the church, doing visitations, attending district meetings, and a thousand other duties that keep him busy and from being bored. Nights are spent in Bible studies and more meetings; and weekends, in preparing sermons, Bible studies, weekly messages, newsletter articles, church maintenance, and whatever else needs to be done in the line of church work.

There is no question that each minister's wife has her own story, and the stories are different depending on the church served, and of course the personality-type of her husband, the pastor. A couple of years ago there was a highly publicized story about the pastor's wife who actually was driven to kill her pastor husband. As authors and pastors' wives, we want to assure our audience that this is not the norm, but at the same time, we are also very aware that there are tensions, pressures, and joys that each pastor's wife must live with on a daily basis.

A pastor's only day off can become a complicated affair, and as co-authors our husbands routinely take different days off. Faith's husband takes Friday off with only funerals and wedding rehearsals that interfere with his plans. My husband used to have Fridays as his day off but soon discovered that was when everyone went into the hospital, so he changed his day off to Thursday. Now everyone goes into the hospital on Thursdays instead! Today is Thursday. Excuse me a moment, the phone just rang. You guessed it (no joking), someone is going into the hospital at 1:00 p.m. Need to change our plans for today.

Pastor call papers also differ. Call papers for Faith's husband state that he must work on all church holidays. My husband's call papers from our church reads that he gets holidays off, e.g., Christmas, Easter, Thanksgiving, etc. Opps! Someone had a sense of humor or lack of knowledge of the pastor's job! Vacation days seem to be designed for funerals, and every pastor will tell you that most funerals occur close to Christmas Eve and Easter. Once I was privy to the conversation of a group of ministers over lunch. They were challenging each other as to who had the most funerals during Christmas week that year. We only had two. The winner had an unseemly number of seven for that week. It is no wonder that those new to the role of "minister's wife" find it overwhelming!

Now-a-days you find that the pastor's wife also has a full time job outside of the home as well. I, as a Lutheran school principal, and Faith, as a Lutheran school teacher, were both advised to have a social life outside of the church. Considering the friendships and network of relatives within any church body, there is no such thing as "confidential". For an unmarried pastor to date someone within the congregation is considered "suicidal"; and like in any large family, jealousies are quick to rise. For example, I was recently told of a person who quit a church drama because she didn't get the lead role in an Easter pageant. She even accused the director (who happened to be the minister's wife), of having favorites even though the part called for a male lead! Yep, just like in any other family, jealousies occur within the church body; especially when it concerns anyone in leadership - especially the minister and his wife (Ma and Pa Church).

If you and your husband have been in ministry for any length of time, you can probably relate to what I have just said and add to it. If you are just entering the ministry with your husband, be prepared. It helps if you are self-sufficient and are comfortable spending time alone. Finding your own niche in ministry helps you to relate better to your husband's job. You are a team, and the minister's wife (first lady of the church) has an important role to play in the church. Like it or not, you were given that role when you married a minister, or as in my case, he decided to become one after we were married! Some women in ministry, for example: a minister's wife, deaconess, or a woman in another position of service and leadership within the church have found the calling to be challenging, rich, and fulfilling. Others have found it to be overwhelming, devastating, and lonely. If you are reading this book out of curiosity, we hope you will find it informative as well as amusing.

Being as it is sometimes difficult to find someone outside of the church with whom to discuss church and personal matters, the purpose of this book is to inform, share, support, and yes, amuse. *Wives Lives: Tales from the Parsonage* is a collection of real life experiences of women in ministry that gives voice and an opportunity to share personal experiences with others, especially those new to this calling, as well as those who are just curious about "people in this position". Many different voices are heard in this book, with a variety of writing styles that illustrate a vast array of experiences. True to qualitative research, the stories are real, but in some instances, names and places have been changed to preserve confidentiality and anonymity. A list of questions for discussion is included at the end of the book for personal reflection and/or discussion.

Wives Lives: Tales from the Parsonage attempts to show, without a doubt, that those in ministry are far from perfect and can be just as "wacky" as the next person; but in all that happens, there is *Christ in the center*. We must find the humor in our lives to fully appreciate

God's mercy!   With our hopes that these stories will lighten your load, renew your spirit, and brighten your day as they have for us,

We Remain Yours in Christ,
Jill Anthony, Ph.D. and Faith Wesolik, Ph.D.

Table of Contents

1

BEGINNINGS

"Where shall I begin, please your Majesty?" He asked. "Begin at the beginning," the King said, very gravely, "and go on till you come to the end: then stop."

- Lewis Carroll

JOB OPENING: MINISTER'S WIFE

I was talking to a fourteen year old the other day and asked what she planned to do after high school.

"I'm going to go to Bible College," she said.

"And what do you plan to study?" I inquired.

"I want to be a minister's wife!" she replied.

Well, to my knowledge they don't offer courses on how to be a minister's wife, but I do remember one person who was advertising for one. It was back at Concordia, when I was studying to be a teacher. A male classmate was planning on graduating in the summer and was entering the mission field in some remote country, probably without electricity and running water, and with lots of mosquitoes. He was bound and determined to take a wife with him when he left. Rumor has it that he asked anyone in a skirt out on a date and then proposed. I don't know how many dates it took, but he finally found someone to apply for 'the job'.

My plans were to teach for the Peace Corps a while, then return home, marry a farmer, have five kids, and raise crops and animals that would never be butchered. Needless to say, none of those plans ever came to fruition except for the fact that I did raise some chickens, a few ducks, and two turkeys that eventually all died of old age. Instead, I married a teacher and we both taught in Lutheran schools for over twenty years, after which my husband became an ordained minister. Overnight I became not only a teacher but 'A minister's wife'! (without any preparatory courses, I might add.)

I thought back on the ministers wives that I was somewhat familiar with beginning with my teen years and Mrs. Hasz. Pastor and Mrs. Hasz immigrated from Germany. She was a large woman who looked like a Haus Frau in her cotton house dresses. She made hot chocolate and home made cookies for the youth group each year when we came back on cold nights from Christmas caroling. She was a quiet woman and wasn't exactly real pretty, but the twinkle in her eyes, 'grandmother' smile, and gentle ways made me like her.

I also remember Lou Anne who rotated meetings for every group we had at our Missouri church. This way she got to know all the people, let them know she cared, and didn't show favoritism. Sounds like a plan to me! Myra, on the other hand, was her husband's 'partner' in ministry. One self-appointed job seemed to be 'to keep the wives of male faculty members in line'. We were required to attend a Bible class at her home once a week, after which she would instruct us on proper care of our husbands and his clothes among other things.

Barb, in Ohio, worked full time as a nurse. This excused her from lots of meetings. (I was never fond of meetings, so that sounded good to me.) She chose the projects she wanted to be involved in, was dressed impeccably, and always knew the right thing to say. Everyone loved Barb.

Then came Dorothy. Dorothy was a widow who had been married to a truck driver for many years before she became 'a Minister's wife'. She requires a paragraph of her own! Her hair was dyed blonde, medium length, and curly. She was short and pleasingly plump and thrived on natural herbs and her own home cooking. Bright, bold colors appealed to Dorothy and rosy cheeks and lips completed her attire. She was a friendly person who liked people and telling jokes (usually not in mixed company), and would throw her head back with a bold laugh. At different times in her life, she did crafts, catering, and wedding cakes. She was very active in her church. Though some might be taken back a little at first by this unconventional minister's wife, there was no pretense about her. What you saw was what you got. I liked Dorothy; she was warm and caring, sincere, and FUN!

I was teaching at a college when my husband received his first full time call to a church. One of the first orders of business was what to call me. I didn't realize that was so important, but I guess it was. They offered Dr. Anthony..

I said, "No, that's what my students call me. You are not my students." They offered Mrs. Anthony.

I said, "No, that's my mother-in-law's name. Just call me Jill." They weren't comfortable with that. After all, I was the minister's wife. (Oh, good grief!) Someone suggested 'Teacher Anthony'. Much too formal. Finally, they offered 'Dr. Jill', and so it has been. My husband and I have been at this church for ten years, and now, occasionally, someone will slip and just call me 'Jill'; mostly the new, young members. And that is fine.

In the beginning, the three Sunday School teachers avoided me like the plague. When I inquired as to the cause for their dislike, I was told that the former minister's wife didn't approve of what they did in Sunday School and was always interfering with 'their job' Once they learned that I wanted nothing to do with Sunday School teaching, they relaxed. I started teaching Sunday School when I was just twelve. I was delighted to be able to finally attend a Sunday morning Bible class for adults!

Unlike Dorothy, I am not a 'party person'. I like people, but am uncomfortable in large gatherings. I have never and do not join or participate in cliques. My place in ministry has been to find what needs to be done that no one else wants to do, and that becomes my mission or 'job'. My defining moment as a minister's wife came at our first Easter at our new church home.   Since this church did not have a choir, I decided to start one - no training or talent required- just like to sing and praise the Lord! I had never directed a church choir before and could not accompany the choir so we used 'canned' music. It worked well. We were a praise choir of six people who sang in unison. I chose to do a Cantata for Easter. How hard could it be? I think you are familiar with the phrase, "Fools rush in where angels fear to tread."

Easter came, and my husband decided on a processional of cross, banner, Bible, acolytes, choir, and minister. Marge was in charge of the acolytes. The question was 'in what order should we process?' No one seemed to know, and I was having a hard time just keeping my choir members in a line at all, not leaving to talk to people as others came in, and not blocking the entrance to the church proper. (This problem continues to this day! It was easier to handle a class of 35 middle grade students!)

Marge asked me, "In what order do we line them up?"

Pulling one my choir members back in line, I said, "I don't know."

A few minutes later, Marge asked again, "Do they follow the choir?"

I replied, "I don't know. You will have to ask Pastor," as I tried to get another choir member away from the church entrance.

It was almost time for church to start, and my husband was still in his office. I am a 'time freak'; my choir members were scattered everywhere, and this was our first major work of praise! Marge asked for the third time, "Should we start now?"

Dragging yet another choir member back in line, I said in a slightly raised, edgy voice, "I don't know. I am not in charge!"

Then I saw it. Marge was the age of my mother. She pursed her lips and turned away with a look that said, "You don't need to be so grumpy about it!" It was a hurt look. Out of my own frustration, I knew I had hurt her feelings and I would need to apologize for my 'tone of voice' right away. But then, my husband finally appeared, we processed in, and it would have to wait until after church.

Church over; choir robes put away, elated choir members sped off to Easter dinner with their families. The Altar Guild was preparing the altar for next Sunday's service. Marge was standing alone near the front of the church. My plan was to privately talk to Marge. I walked down the aisle and sheepishly approached her.

"Marge," I said. She turned with that motherly stern look still on her face. The altar guild ladies also stopped their work and turned to watch AND LISTEN! Obviously, she had shared her hurt and disappointment with the new minister's wife, and they were going to listen and make a judgment if I should be banned from the church or whatever they did with wayward minister wives. My plan was to privately talk to Marge. It was clear that wasn't going to happen.

"Marge," I began, "I need to apologize for my tone of voice just before church started. I have never directed a church choir before. I didn't know anymore than you what order we should process in. I didn't even keep my choir members in line. I didn't mean to sound gruff or disrespectful to you. Church was about to start, my husband was no where to be seen, and I was just frustrated. I hope you can forgive me."

That was one of the hardest, most embarrassing little speeches I have ever had to make (especially before an audience!) Marge, with a smile on her face instantly threw her arms around me and said, "I understand. I forgive you." The altar guild smiled and went back to their work and chatting. That act of contrition on my part not only gained me forgiveness but a group of senior ladies that have remained close friends and a mother substitute for me over the years. On that day, I truly became a member of the congregation. I was their minister's wayward wife.

In conclusion. I think each minister's wife is unique with different gifts to offer a church. It is up to her, in her own way and time, to discover her place within that congregation. I'm not sure that is something that can really be taught. It's about you, what's in your heart, the people of the church, and daily prayer to God that you 'do more good than harm' in your new family, and the humility to apologize when needed. I cannot over emphasize the latter. Little 'things' left uncorrected can do more harm than a major faux pas that's been confessed. A true act of contrition can give you a warm and loving family for life. To God be the glory!

"For all those things My hand has made,
And all those things exist," Says the Lord.
"But on this one will I look: On him who is poor and of a contrite
*   spirit,*
And who trembles at My word." Isaiah 66: 2

THE BEAM OF LIGHT

It was with a heavy heart that I sat in one of the back pews of the church, taking in my surroundings. It wasn't so much that I feared the new role I would be cast in, that of the pastor's wife. It was more the idea of joining a denomination whose practice of the Christian faith was stilted, formal, and somewhat lifeless. That was my perception at the time. Over the years, the Lord had shown me the meaning of true freedom in Christ, and I was not about to be put back into a straitjacket once again. I was looking for authenticity in worship, and a place where our walk with God could be safely shared. Those precious moments when God speaks through scripture or through the words of a hymn or through the kind words of a friend had always been a huge encouragement to me, and to share such experiences with brothers and sisters in Christ was part of what 'church' meant to me.

We had traveled a long way, my husband and I, to bring us to this place in our faith journey. We came from a denomination where the Bible was not honored as God's true revelation to mankind, and where moral principles were twisted to 'fit modern times'. We just could not stay. For a few years we floated in and out of various churches, and always in the back of my husband's mind was the idea that God was calling him to the ministry. Finally a friend invited him to his church and he excitedly told him of the good work that was being done there, the wonderful pastor, and the biblically sound stand they were taking. Not only that, but they were interested in supporting my husband's application for ministry. There is nothing like a passionate Christian to attract others, and so here we were, attending our first service.

The liturgy was strange, the hymn books were old, and around me were a sea of strangers. I felt weary and discouraged. As I looked around at the traditional brick edifice with its rectangular sanctuary and vaulted ceiling, I started to notice the beautiful stained glass windows. Each one featured a different symbol of the Christian faith - the dove representing the Holy Spirit at Christ's baptism in the Jordan River; the cross and crown representing His crucifixion and ultimate ascension into heaven; the sheaves of wheat reminding us that the harvest is plentiful and that mankind desperately needs the Savior. As I admired the colors, intricate workmanship, and message depicted in each symbol, suddenly the morning sun burst into the room through those colored panes of stained glass. The rays of the sun shone directly on me as I was seated in the pew. I was enveloped in light. I felt the comfort of the sunshine as it enfolded me with warmth. I closed my eyes and basked in its blinding brilliance. It was then that I knew without a shadow of a doubt that the Lord was present and would never leave me; that He would see me through any hurdles I might have to face. I needed to let go of my circumstances and my fears and trust in the One who is forever trustworthy.

A deep calm came over me. In that moment I knew we would go into ministry. We might not be traveling an easy road, but the Lord of all creation, the One who made the earth and the planets, the One who died for me on the cross, that same Lord also had a personal interest in this lowly creature and would look after me, and help me navigate those ecclesiastical waters by his guiding light.

It has now been 16 years since the Lord gave me that special assurance of His love. I have seen His faithfulness time after time as He has poured light into the dark recesses of my soul. The verse given to me as a new member in the church was so appropriate.

"The Lord is my light and my salvation; whom shall I fear? The Lord is the stronghold of my life; of whom shall I be afraid?"
(Psalm 27:1)

WHO IS THAT CUTE GUY IN THE WINDOW?

The wind and snow pelted my face as I walked that long city block with my mother on a cold December Saturday afternoon long ago. Christmas shopping was fun, but looking for mom's new Christmas shoes was not! We finally got to Smith's shoe store, and upon entering, I must admit that it felt good to have a respite from the cold wind.

As we entered the store, I noticed a cute young shoe clerk emerging from the store window which he had been decorating. He noted that I was entering the store as he exited the window, and I must confess that suddenly shoe shopping with my mother became very interesting. 'WOW,' I thought to myself, as I noted his trendy green suit. 'This guy really knows how to dress!'

He immediately approached my mother and me and asked if he could help us. "Yes," I heard myself say, as I quickly engaged him in a conversation. Even at the tender age of seventeen, I sensed that he kind of liked me. Luckily, that day my mother seemed to take an extra long time to choose the shoes she was going to purchase, but for me, time seemed to fly. Finally, she made her selections, and it was time for us to leave the store.

Frank and I had engaged in a conversation which I still can clearly remember. I had revealed to him that I played a clarinet in my high school band, and he made a 'quirky' joke about clarinet players. As mother and I exited Smith's Shoe Store, Frank's very best friend entered. Why it was Bob W. who had been my friend since our grade school days! He and I exchanged a few friendly words as we exited the store, and I said a final 'goodbye' to that cute shoe clerk.

As Christmas and its festivities came and went, that cute shoe clerk in the store window faded from my mind until one night late in January. I was studying that night at the breakfast room table when the phone rang. I answered the phone, and to my surprise, the caller identified himself as Frank, the shoe clerk from Smith's Shoe Store. He asked me if I remembered him, and then asked if I would go to a party with him that Bob's girlfriend was having on Saturday evening. I was not sure that my father, a conservative minister's son, would allow me to go out with someone that he did not know. However, after some persistence, I was able to persuade him that Frank was Bob's friend, and it would be OK.

The party was a blast, and as we danced and conversed, Frank admitted that he had asked his friend ,"Who is that girl, and where does she live?" My inklings had been right. He did like me enough to find the pertinent information that led to our first date! As time went on, I discovered that my new friend was from a different church denomination. I knew that even though I really liked him a lot that our friendship would have to remain just that. Nevertheless, I knew that I really liked that cute shoe clerk who had emerged from the store window. He was ambitious, believed in working, and had a great personality!! He had everything that I admired in a person . . . .what more was there to look for?

As the year went by, we engaged in many conversations related to our religions. Back and forth, back and forth, back and forth; yes, our serious conversations turned into doctrinal debates. We debated over many things. One April day I realized that my friendly 'acquaintance' had become my boyfriend and we were falling in love! I, having been born into a long time Lutheran family, and he into a family with a long time background in another church denomination, knew that if we were to marry, we would have to have these doctrinal issues worked out.

Frank, who was a sociology major, had learned how important it was to have major issues settled before marriage. However, I knew that I could not, and would not abdicate my beliefs. The great thing was that we were both Christians: believers in Jesus Christ as our Lord and Savior. This major belief was our commonality, and we never debated that we were saved by Jesus.

I often thought about Martin Luther in those days, and asked myself why he had turned everything upside down, when he only wanted to reform the evils within the church of that time that were in need of change. The reward for me was that these differences really brought me into a close relationship with the Lord. I prayed, read my Bible, and even reread that blue Catechism that I once had spent so many hours memorizing for my conformation classes. I grew only to be more committed as a Christian and to my Lutheran beliefs.

Yes, God did work in miraculous ways. My determined boyfriend decided to take church membership classes, and upon the end of his first class, joined my beloved Lutheran Church. However, he still wanted to learn more, and he took the information class again, and asked question after question about the church's doctrine. Then finally his questions were answered one fall evening after class as he drove his green Ford Falcon toward his home. He must have been meditating on what he had been reading in Scripture and learning in class that evening.

As he drove into the sunset, he was suddenly awakened to the Gospel message that we are 'saved by grace through faith in Jesus Christ, and not by our works.' As he tells the story, the message came to him loud and strong, and he was overwhelmed with joy with the realization of his salvation. God had moved his 'head knowledge' to 'heart knowledge'. This was indeed the conversion moment that has stayed with him the rest of his life, and by which he has lived and shared with thousands thereafter.

Yes, God does answer prayer, and sometimes not only gives us what we ask for, but much more. My boyfriend later became my husband and has served over thirty-five years as a Lutheran minister. Our greatest lesson has been that as God's children, He has called each of us to serve according to His plan. All things, and all of life's happenings are a part of His greater plan for us, and we are indeed in the palm of his hands at all times. True, God will permit us to be challenged, but will give us no more than we can endure. To God be the glory!

"With men this is impossible, but with God all things are possible."
Matthew 19:26

SEM WIVES LIVES

"Let a woman learn in silence with all submission." I Timothy 2:11
"And we know that all things work together for good to those who
love God, to those who are called according to His purpose."
Romans 8:28

Many church members have no idea about the sacrifices seminary wives and their husbands make in order to answer the call the Lord has placed in their hearts to serve Him in ministry. Often the young couples come to the seminary directly out of college with heavy school loans that they already have accumulated, without a full-time job, and sometimes too poor to eat nourishing food or to buy needed clothing. Seminaries often provide both food and clothing banks for those who are in need of help. The following short vignettes are real-life instances written to help depict the sacrifices that are made in order to follow God's call.

FROZEN STIFF

It all seemed to come at once. I was a newly-wed, a new teacher, lived in a new town, and also had become a Sem wife. What more could a young wife want or need? All of the seminarians were in the same boat, study, work, eat, sleep, and don't spend any money! Money just wasn't there for any of us. Being so young, no one really cared, and we did many things together. Many of us lived in public housing close to the seminary. When we got together we shared jokes and secrets that only we could enjoy. As I reflect on that life so many years ago, I can recall a number of wonderful stories. The following is just an example of many incidents that will give you a sample of our lives.

One Monday morning as I was on my way to work, I noticed something hanging on the clothesline of my fried Sara, who lived a few houses up the block from me. She had washed her husband's white surplus and hung it on the clothes line. The only thing wrong with her plan was that it was January! To my dismay, the gown that she had washed and hung out to dry the night before was frozen stiff! In fact, it looked like a white-washed wall board hanging on the clothesline swaying back and forth in the wind taking on the form of a frozen ghost. Yes, we were all young, and poor, and 'dumb' in those days, and often learned our lessons the hard way. However, the good thing was, the Lord blessed us all with a sense of humor!

HOUSE BUNNIES

Psalm 132:15 I will abundantly supply what she needs; I will give the poor all the food they need.

One of the couples we knew during our seminary days was older than the rest of us, and even had three or perhaps four children. As was common to all seminary couples, we had to find ways to manage our meager earnings in order to provide the necessary funds for a house, food, clothing, and college. Our friends, Tom and Mary had found the perfect solution to their monetary problems: they resorted to raising bunnies in their attic. They figured that raising bunnies served three purposes: they were perfect pets for their children; after being fattened-up, the bunnies were then served as meat for their evening meals; and the fur pelts could be used to make their children coats and hats.

This all seemed like a perfectly good plan, but the aroma those little bunnies sent down the flight of stairs into their home has never escaped from my mind to this day! Enough said, OK? With those special times still lingering in my memory, this couple was resourceful, and did get through the rigorous and hard times presented to them during their seminary days and are off serving the Lord in a place where He has called them. As I remember this story, I am reminded of a truth all of us learned in those days: our heavenly Father faithfully supplies for all our daily needs to be met.

DATE NIGHTS

It's Friday again, and of course it was our date night. Let's see whose home are we scheduled to meet at this evening? Yes, it was Dick and Anne's. You see, date nights for us who were seminarians were potluck get- togethers, and it was my turn to bring the dessert. As I sat and ate my piece of toast, I thought for a while, and decided to bring that delicious cream cheese blueberry pie that my mother often made for special occasions. Yes, I would take that recipe out of my box where it was safely stored.

As the day progressed I went to the grocery store after my school day was over, and bought the necessary ingredients. With one exception, everything was available. However, today the store was out of fresh blueberries, so I decided to substitute frozen blueberries for the fresh ones called for in the recipe. I was really happy that this was the ideal dessert for a working woman to make in a flash so that it could be ready for dinner. All seemed to be going well as I mixed the ingredients in my new mixer, and finally it was time to add the blueberries. *I had defrosted them as I mixed the other ingredients*, and now they were ready to go. Wow, I was really beginning to like this cooking responsibility that married life had brought into my life! It was finally time to add the berries and place the dessert in the refrigerator so that my new husband would be surprised when he came home from his part-time job as a shoe clerk.

'One-two-three- magic!' I thought, except something terribly wrong was happening. My dessert was turning a dreadful color of gray. 'This did not look at all like the dessert that my mother makes,' I thought to myself. What had I done wrong? I quickly picked up the phone and called my dear mother to ask her what to do, only to find out that I had not drained the frozen blueberries because the recipe did not call for draining them.

She explained that because they were not fresh berries, the juice leaked into the mixture and discolored the creamy white color into a gray shade that looked horrible. However, she did assure me that the pie would still taste delicious. I absolutely had no choice but to take that horrible gray dessert to the potluck dinner that night. The truth was, I could not afford to buy more ingredients, and I had promised to bring the dessert. The evening was not as dismal as I thought it would be, and as I joked about my terrible mistake, everyone had something to tease me about for the next three years of our Seminary life.

I WANT TO GO HOME!

'Ugg!' I thought to myself. 'It's Sunday again, and church is over for another week.' Several of the couples our age were standing in the Narthex making plans once again on where they would meet for lunch. They eagerly made their plans, with me in the presence, but unintentionally left my husband and me out. In those days, I often asked, "Why me, Lord?" I had always had friends and family close to me, and now I was in this strange new land with my newly ordained husband, and I just didn't fit in. What am I doing wrong? The weeks moved so slowly, and I was alone, ever so alone.

My father had just been diagnosed with a life-threatening disease. My grandmother was suffering from dementia. I had recently become pregnant, and I had my precious first-born to take care of. 'What would I do without Zachary?' I often thought as I watched him sleep. I wondered how in the world I could have another child as perfect as he. Day in and day out my baby boy and I spent time together, learning to talk, toddle, walk, and then run. This was indeed a bittersweet time.

Although my mom and I talked often, we couldn't see each other because both of us were tied down with our new responsibilities. My husband was very busy in his first call to be a minister, and also to be a part of the life in the community. In fact, after a year, he was elected as the Outstanding Young Man in our state. Wow, what an honor! Yet, I was bathed in loneliness, and often asked myself if this was really what all ministers' wives experience, or was I just not doing it right?

The first Thanksgiving came with Christmas soon to follow and then there was Easter. No, we can't go home, my husband is a pastor, and has more obligations during this time of the year than any other. Again all of the young couples in church were making their holiday plans of either having their family members come to celebrate with them or they were going home to be with their loved ones. Why many of these folks even had their families right there, but it's a family day and no one would think of asking us to share time with them. How wonderful for them and how lonely it was for us that first year. As I now reflect back over the years, it was within this time frame I realized that NO, we could not go home this year, or for any of the next forty years to come for the holidays.

The aching loneliness of being a pastor's wife had never dawned on me. How would any lay person realize that although a pastor's wife (PW) has many beautiful acquaintances, it's nearly impossible to have a close friend in the church. You are there to minister, befriend, and share your beloved husband unselfishly with all the members of your congregation. But somehow, you are not able to really embrace one or two people to be your closest friends.

I'd been advised that it's just not fair to select one person over another. And, to make matters worse, I should not confide anything, for you must be able to trust that your private information does not spread through the grape-vine that is so prevalent in every church. I actually have equated the position of a PW to that of a politician's wife! The big difference is that they can, at some point, see an end to their life's dilemma; I could not.

Sadly, this is one of the negatives of being a PW. I learned early that loneliness must be dealt with. The beautiful hymn that has run through my mind many times and delivered me over the years, was one that my sainted grandmother sang often as she gazed out the window: "What a Friend we Have in Jesus, all our sins and grief to bear! What a privilege to carry, everything to God in prayer." The lesson that I've learned is that I am not alone. My best friend is Jesus, and He is always present.

And He said, "My Presence will go with you, and I will give you rest." Exodus 33:14

2

GOD IN NATURE

"Posterity will some day laugh at the foolishness of modern materialistic philosophy. The more I study nature, the more I am amazed at the Creator."

- Louis Pasteur

A WINTER CONFESSION

Yesterday, the snow melted, and tufts of green grass could be seen once again to our cat's delight. Two red-winged black birds (the true harbingers of spring) appeared on the fence, and cardinals sang their love songs from the peak of the apple tree. You could smell spring in the air.

This morning we woke up to a winter wonderland with a four inch coverlet of snow and another four to eight inches promised before night fall. "Look's like Bible class will be cancelled this morning," I said to my husband. Our congregation is small, but most members belong to one of the seven Bible classes he offers each week. Psalms and Prayers consist of mostly senior citizens who are afraid to drive in bad weather. Nevertheless, he proceeded to get the snow blower out of the shed to clear our long driveway before leaving for church. If the snow got any deeper, our snow blower would not be able to handle it.

I got dressed, cleared my buried car of snow, and prepared for a trip to the park. In addition to two Siamese cats, we have two American Eskimos. The latter live for days such as this! It was already 7:00 a.m., and I had to move quickly. There is a metro park about ten minutes drive from our home. The park rangers open the entryway at 8:00 a.m. each morning. However, near the bowling alley, there is a back entrance to the hiking trail which is always available by foot. It is at this entrance that I take my dogs before the park is officially opened. I am a minister's wife, but I break the rules: the rule that says, 'Thou shalt keep thy dogs on a hand held leash': hence my early departure. There is a $50.00 fine if your dogs aren't on a leash. I flirt with crime and poverty in order to give them a chance to 'run free'!

The dogs eagerly jump in the car, and we proceed down the road. Nearing the bowling alley, I am pleased to see no other cars near the trail entrance. I plunge forward hoping my car doesn't get stuck in the ever deepening snow. Kodie is the first to eagerly bound out of the car (no leash). Haley, I attach a long leash to, then let her run free. The air is brisk, but not cold (if you keep moving). I check the trail for footprints. Yes, someone has beaten me to the park. No dogs, and he has returned and left. Yes! The park is ours!

Kodie (looking much like an arctic wolf) and Haley (smaller like an arctic fox) are rolling and wrestling in the snow like two growling wolverines. I smile as my 'children' play and proceed down the wooded path with them leading the way. Snow is falling steadily, but softly brushes my cheek. A cathedral of tall trees with 'cotton' covered branches and an occasional 'wedding cake' stump line the trail. The path is clear with the exception of one set of footprints going and then returning. Squirrels and rabbits, which are generally busy in the brush, are conspicuously absent on this day. There are no birds to scold us from above. All is quiet except for the soft sound of padding feet. I marvel at God's creation (He does such nice work!), and I am more at peace in the woods than anywhere else on earth. I feel close to God here. I reflect in the quiet and revel in its beauty.

This peacefulness invariably leads to reflection. Today, the thought is, 'When did God create snow?' We picture the Garden of Eden like a Polynesian paradise. Did Adam and Eve ever see snow? I decide that taking all into consideration, location and clothing (or lack thereof) most likely they did not see snow. Too bad! Then (with much bias) maybe that garden wasn't quite so perfect after all to have missed this beauty.)

I am awakened from my thoughts by the sound of Haley's barking. She has managed to get her long trailing leash tangled in a bush. We have been walking for about one half hour. Kodie has frozen snow balls hanging from his trousers (the long hair extending from the rumps of long haired dogs), legs, and chest. He stops every few feet now to chew at the cumbersome orbs that sway back and forth with each step he takes. Chewing only makes them adhere all the more. He will need a hot bath to remove them. We head back to the car refreshed and ready to meet the new day. The dogs will sleep well once the snowballs are removed. As we approach the car, I detect a waif of something good. What is it and where is it coming from? I turn in the direction of the smell and notice the Harvest Café now with several cars outside. Breakfast is being served. Time to go home and cook up some 'vitals'.

After some skidding and rocking the car, I am able to get it back on the road and head for home. The dogs got to run and do their 'doggie thing', and I have avoided capture and a fine for yet another day. God is Good! What a beautiful start to a new day. "Good Morning, God."

"Purge me with hyssop, and I shall be clean;
Wash me, and I shall be whiter than snow." Ps. 51:7

WHAT I LEARNED FROM A ROBIN

"CHIRP, CHIRP, CHIRP," came the sound from the dining room.

"Oh, no," I said running to the next room. "Lock the dogs in the den. Sonny must have caught a bird."

Turning the corner, I saw Sonny, our Siamese cat, deposit a fledgling robin on the floor. This bird must have been the poster bird for 'bird brains', because no sooner had Sonny put her down then the bird began beating her wings demanding to be fed. How could a bird that was at least two weeks old think that a cat could be her mother?

"Get the cat carrier;" I called to my husband as I picked up the squawking bird. "It's on the shelf in the utility room."

"What are you going to do?" he asked returning with the carrier.

I gently placed the bird in the carrier and gave Sonny a treat (in place of the bird dinner that she obviously was not going to have). I replied that I had to take a look outside.

Once out, I looked and listened for a frantic mother bird flying about and the sound of other fledglings. When young robins are about half grown they no longer fit in the nest. At this point, they end up on the ground where the parents watch over them and feed them until their tail and wing feathers grow in enough that they are able to fly high in the trees. It is a very dangerous time in their young lives because they are very easy prey, not to mention that the loud chirping sounds signal where they are hiding.

"Could you find the mother?" My husband asked somewhat hopefully.

"Not a sign of a robin anywhere," I replied. "There is no telling where Sonny found her."

"What are you going to do?" he asked skeptically.

"No choice but to feed her, since I can't find her family."

"I was afraid you were going to say that. We already have two dogs and two cats. We don't need another pet."

"Robin is a wild thing. She needs to be free. I will feed her until she can be on her own."

"Can you do that?"

"Sure, if she will eat for me."

"Great!" came the none so excited reply. "What are you going to feed her?"

"Well for now, all I have is bread and scrambled eggs."

"Can they eat that?"

"Well, it's not their favorite, but it will serve until I can get to the store. She is really hungry!" I replied as the bird continued to drown out any and all conversation. She wanted to be fed NOW!

I soaked a little rye bread in milk, placed it on a tooth pick and gently poked it down the gapping, demanding mouth.

CHIRP (more), CHIRP (more), CHIRP(I want more) came the ravenous reply.

"Well, let's try a little scrambled eggs. I think I read about that somewhere."

Robin hungrily devoured whatever I offered. Seeing a small bulge on the side of her throat, I returned the bird to the carrier with the reassurance that I would return with something more appetizing.

"Now what are going to do?" asked my dubious husband.

"Birds eat many times their weight each day and need to be fed every hour."

"Great! As if you don't have enough to do. Where are you going now?"

"To the store."

"Why?"

"To get worms." It always struck me funny that if you live near a body of water, no matter how small, that you can always get bait at the local 'Stop and Go'. Going a block up the street, I entered the store and headed to the cooler where one could find night crawlers, crickets, red swigglers, and meal worms on the bottom shelf below the milk and 'people food'. I got red swigglers and meal worms at $2.00 a box. The next day, I went grocery shopping and picked up blue berries and Bing cherries. Robins seldom ever eat seeds, but I remember their gorging themselves on my cherry tree before the cherries were even ripe and getting caught under netting while feasting on blueberries. These birds have expensive tastes!

Robin, not an original name I must admit, but appropriate, loved the chow but was not happy with her living quarters. Not wanting to spend lots of money on a bird cage that would have limited use and because it was costing almost $4.00 a day to feed this bird, I decided to check out our local Good Will Store. There was not one bird cage in the entire store; however, someone had just brought in a guinea pig cage. Saved! Once home, I attached a long dowel which served as a perch, and I introduced Robin to her new temporary quarters. As she lighted on the perch, I could see the guinea pig cage was the best thing for her considering her long legs and long wing span. A regular bird cage would not have been nearly wide enough for her stretching exercises which she began to do almost immediately.

Robin reminded me hourly when it was time for her to eat. She woke up with the sun and I put her to bed around 8:00 p.m. One day I saw her scratching at the newspaper and picking up the wax paper on the bottom of the cage with her beak. So far so good, but now I was stumped. How would I go about teaching a robin how to find worms and find her own food? To make it more difficult, we hadn't had rain for three weeks. The ground was dry and the worms would be deep.

While I pondered this question, I continued to feed Robin but now with a pair of tweezers. She was reaching out to grab the worms, but I kept dropping them! Robin watched me drop the worms time after time. Were these worm pieces wigglier than the others? They seemed short enough but then they stretched themselves out and kept moving each time I neared Robin's mouth, making it impossible for me to get them in the hungry 'hole'. Out of desperation, Robin began picking them off the bottom of the cage.

When Robin's tail and flying feathers grew in, I put Robin's cage outside and opened the cage door. It was breathtaking to see her fly out and up into the tree close to the house. She continued to call to me each hour upon which I would go out and call 'Robin' for another three days. She delighted us by landing on my head or my husband's shoulder, and we took turns feeding her, after which she flew back into her tree. One day she landed on the ground, and I began putting the meal worms on the ground. She quickly gobbled them up. Meal worms and cherries were her favorite foods! Soon Robin began staying on the ground hiding under the strawberry plants and running out on the longest most slender legs I've ever seen on a bird. She'd eat her food then hide again.

Robin could now fly and eat on her own. She needed only to learn how to find her food and take her rightful place as a wild bird. Another week or so and she would be on her own. The joy I felt just watching her made my heart sing. Ninety percent of all wild birds hatched do not survive. However, if they can make it past the first year, they generally live their natural life span. Now that robin was free and outside, I prayed daily that God would protect her. It looked as though we were going to beat the odds. Then one day, I heard her chirp and looked outside as a hawk swooped down and soared off with her in his mouth. All that was left of the last wonderful thirteen days of sharing her life were feathers on the ground. I was inconsolable and had a hard talk with God.

Filled with anger and pain, with tears running down my face, I demanded to know "WHY". Why didn't God protect her? I had trusted Him to do so. Why did He bring her into my life, just to have her die an awful death? She was so perfect and so innocent, and I loved her. Was it too much to ask? WHY? Would it have destroyed 'some vast eternal plan' just to let this little bird live?! God had brought me through other disasters and hard times in life, but this wasn't about me. It was about an innocent little bird. It just wasn't fair! Where was the justice in this? For the first time in my life, I was angry with God. I know better than to question God in His wisdom, but the pain at that moment seemed more than I could bear. You might say, "But it was just a little bird! You only had it for thirteen days. " And I would reply, " but such is the power of a parent's love."(adoptive or not)

A year has passed. Spring has returned once again, and thoughts return to Robin. As I tell her story, tears hit my keyboard as I type. I look at the paragraph above "Filled with anger and pain . . .".Aren't these the same feelings and words that parents experience when they lose an infant, a child. Wasn't God's own son brought into this world just to die? Was Robin sent to help me experience and understand the pain others feel at the loss of a child; how my daughter-in-law felt when my grandson died shortly after birth? How God, our Father, must have felt at the death of Jesus? Slowly, I begin to understand.

Sometimes it is difficult to find meaning in life, but whereas we see small glimpses of life, God sees the whole, overall picture. Like a puzzle piece that doesn't seem to belong, in the end we find that the puzzle couldn't be completed without that particular piece. I take a break from writing and walk outside to enjoy the fresh air. I am amazed to see my back yard covered with robins gobbling up the worms after a spring rain. Noticing the abundance of robins in my yard, my neighbor comes over and comments, "What's with all the robins? Have you ever seen this many before?"

"No," I reply. "I have never seen so many robins in my yard before." Where last year, I had one, now there are many: too many to count. The Psalmist reminds us that 'Weeping may endure for a night, But joy comes in the morning.' (Psalm 30: 5) And so it is this day as I complete my puzzle with understanding, and enjoy the wonderful sight before me. Gazing at the multiple of robins before me, I am filled with joy! Thank you, Jesus.

3

RELATIONSHIPS

*A wife once asked her minister husband to help with the dishes.
"That isn't man's work!" he said. "That's not what the Bible says,"
she replied. " . . . and I will wipe Jerusalem as a man wipeth a
dish, wiping it, and turning it upside down."*

II Kings 21:13

THE RIGHT HAND

I was working on a mural that I was painting on the back wall of our church's fellowship hall. It was to be a life-sized picture of Jesus walking through a garden with a stone wall and large trees. I had been working on the mural some each day for about two weeks, and it was finally nearing completion. On this particular day, I had spent two hours on the face of Jesus, and now it was time to work on His hands. The sketch from which I was working showed hands in a position that I wasn't sure I could duplicate on a concrete wall and do them justice.

Some of our senior ladies had just finished their Psalm and Prayers Bible study and gathered around to check out 'the mess I was making'. Hearing my dilemma, Marge suggested that I just paint Jesus with his hands in his pockets. Actually, I have used tricks like this before in order to avoid having to tackle troublesome hands that could end up ruining an entire piece of art. But, I wasn't sure pockets had been invented yet in the time of Jesus. Also, the hands played an important part in the message that I wanted the mural to present. I decided to make at least the right hand open- the easiest position to paint. Seeing that the figure of Jesus was life sized, I decided to make my job a little easier still by using someone's hands as an outline.

Five ladies gathered around so that I could see their hands. Since Jesus was 6'2" in the mural, I would need a large hand. I looked at all the hands and chose the largest. My model looked at her hands in comparison to the others there and with a kind of sadness in her voice, she said, "I have the largest hands here, and look at how wrinkled and worn they look." Her comments brought to mind a story that I once heard of another pair of hands.

The story goes that there was once a man who had two sons. When he died, his estate was to be divided between the two; however, the estate wasn't very large. Both sons wanted to go to college and study art, but there was hardly enough to pay the tuition for one. The older son offered to stay at home and work the farm to help put his younger brother through college. When the one graduated, he would then in turn work to allow his older brother to attend college. Four years went by, and the younger son graduated with honors from college. He had become a fine artist.

He returned home in order that his older brother could then benefit from a college education; however, the oldest son sadly declined. Holding out his hands, the younger could see that four years of hard labor had left his brother's hands badly scarred, calloused, and arthritic. He could no longer manage the fine delicate movements necessary for detailed art work. Realizing the sacrifice his brother had made in order to enable him to go to college, the younger brother did the only thing that he knew to do; he created an etching of his brother's hands

Many people may not know the name of this artist, but most are familiar with his brother's hands. They are the famous 'Praying Hands' often seen in Christian art, or so the story goes, and the name of the artist is Albrecht Durer. It has been many years since I heard the story, and I don't know if it is true; but I'd like to think that it is.

After the ladies left, I labored another two hours on the one hand, thinking about my model's comments. Like many others in this church, her name could have been Dorcas for all that she does for others and her hard work for our church. How appropriate it was that I was using her hand for Jesus. Marilyn's hand 'is the right hand of Jesus'. The thought lingered and it occurred to me that maybe that's exactly what Jesus expects of us all, **to be His hands in ministry.**

Wherefore , my beloved brethern, let every man be swift to hear, slow to speak, slow to wrath: But Be ye doers of the word, and not hearers only. . . James 1:19 -22.

CONFLICT IN THE FAMILY, PERSONALLY SPEAKING

"Be ye angry, and sin not: let not the sun go down upon your wrath: Let all bitterness, and wrath, and anger and clamor, and evil speaking, be put away from you, with all malice:
Eph. 4:26

It happens like this. One Sunday you notice that Mr. and Mrs. Jones are not in church. They are generally regular in attendance so it catches your attention. Then they are not there the next week. Maybe they are on vacation. The third week you call to see if they are sick, and are just given a lame excuse as to why they haven't been in church. More time passes, and the minister gives them a call and/or visits. He learns that the reason is that another member (knowingly or unknowingly) offended them in some way, so they have transferred their membership to another church without discussing the situation. In our church, this most often occurs to those who have only been members for a year or less. They may have had bad experiences in another church that has left them gun shy. Sometimes, it may just be someone's personality that annoys them; they may not realize that we are all sinners, even in the church.

A church is like a large family, and like any family, there is bound to be disagreement and conflict from time to time. This in itself is not necessarily bad, but how conflict is handled (or not) can be. God in his Word tells us not to sin in our anger. Recently I was asked to serve our church district as an Ambassador of Reconciliation. I wasn't sure what all this entailed, but in the words of our District President, it meant 'a free, all expenses paid trip to St. Louis' where I would join a host of others being trained in reconciliation. Always interested in learning something new, I said, "sure". I have since learned to be more suspicious when offered 'free trips!'

What followed was three intense days and nights of training led by Ken Sande and Ted Kober, the founders of Peacemaker Ministries. I personally don't like conflict. I tend to deny that a problem exists ('no big deal') or run from it (a coward at heart). Others may deal with conflict by meeting it head on, more of a fight than flight approach. However, in Matthew 18; 15-17, God gives us guidelines for how to handle conflict in a God pleasing manner. This is the basis for Christian Reconciliation when those involved want to restore harmony in a relationship.

Since being trained, I have been asked twice thus far to be part of a team ministering to a church in conflict. To me, this is scary business. Remember, I am the one who prefers to run away! In each situation, 'The Peacemaker' principles were first taught. Afterwards, 'ambassadors' were available to coach those in conflict through the reconciliation process.

I regularly pray diligently that God 'take the helm' in giving us the words that lead to reconciliation.

I was a little more confident at the second church than at the first, but I don't know if I am the best person for this job. As the saying goes, "All I can do is to do my best (as trained) and give God the rest." What I do know is that I can no longer run away from conflict unless it is truly the best approach given the circumstances. So, why am I sharing all this information with you?

1. If you are a member of a Lutheran Church Missouri Synod (LCMS), you may contact your District President for further

information about Ambassadors for Reconciliation.

2. If you are a member of another church denomination, you may want to contact Peacemaker Ministries.

3. Curious, you may purchase books from Peacemaker Ministries.

4. There is also a Bible study on personal peacemaking: "Blessed Are the Peacemakers" (2004) by the Ambassadors of Reconciliation (www.HisAoR.org)

Whether you are a part of an Ambassador team or not, to be well versed in ways to handle conflict, personal or other, in a God pleasing manner is very instrumental in bringing harmony and peace into your personal life. If you are a person in leadership and/or a minister's wife, I especially recommend that you become familiar with Peacemaker materials. I am glad I have had the opportunity to do this, barring 'the free trip to St.. Louis'!

MURDER BY MAIL!

It was almost Christmas, and Pop was expecting his annual Christmas box from his grandson's family who lived out of state. He was more than a little anxious about this gift. More than all the others he had received over the years. His anxiety was confirmed when he went to gather the mail and discovered a shoebox sized package caked and dripping with blood!

Now that I have your attention, let's back up for a moment.

Pop loved feeding the birds. In fact, he was so good at it that the black capped chickadees would even eat out of his hand. It was this love of birds that prompted us to purchase a birdcage, canary, and all the trimmings for Pop for his birthday almost ten years ago. However, the little bird had recently died of old age, leaving the kitchen spot by the sunny window silent and void of cheer. We offered to buy him another canary, but he vehemently refused.

"No bird could replace Tweety", he insisted; "I am now too old to be bothered with cleaning a cage and all the fuss that goes with having a pet. And besides, birds are meant to fly free. I still have all my outside friends."

Still, I was bothered by Pop not having a friend 'inside his house' to keep him company. After some thought, I finally came up with the perfect pet for Pop so that he wouldn't be quite so alone. For twenty-five cents, I purchased an official pet carrying box from the pet store, filled it with soft bedding, instructions on how to teach the new pet how to roll over, gave the pet a kiss and a pat, and placed it in the box which I sealed for safety. Along with the new pet, I enclosed some gloves and a muffler, home made cookies, raspberry preserves, and a book on birds. That done, my husband took the package to the UPS store so that it would arrive quickly and in plenty of time for Christmas. We phoned Pop that night and told him to expect a new pet any day: the beginning of his anxiety. We assured him that it wasn't another bird, that it would travel safely in its carrier, and that he shouldn't worry. And now this!

Fearing what he would find inside the unopened box of Christmas gifts, Pop immediately called his grandson in Missouri, who quickly passed the phone to me.

"The package arrived, and it's all dripping with blood! I think the animal inside is dead! Did you have anything else in the box with the pet? I don't know if I should open the box or just bury it! What kind of animal is it?"

The 'blood' had me puzzled. Then after a moment's reflection, I asked Pop to check the 'blood' for something that looked like seeds.

"Seeds?" he asked.

"Yes," I said. "Come back and tell me if there are seeds in the 'blood', and I'll explain.

"OK, if you say so," he replied.

In a moment he came back. "Yes, there are seeds in the blood. Tell me what this is all about. Is the animal O.K.?"

"Yes, the animal is O.K." I said, trying to keep from laughing. "I placed a jar of raspberry preserves in the box, and I believe that your new pet may have broken the jar trying to get to the berries. I am sure he is O.K., but you need to get him out of the box now. He has had enough excitement for a while.

"Is he in a cage?" he asked, fearful that the creature would begin running loose breaking other things in the house.

"Yes, it is in a carrying box."

"What do I feed it?"

"Instructions are in the box with him, but he would probably liked being placed in a potted plant."

"Potted plants! Not my potted plants!

My husband and I strained to hear as the outer 'blood draped' paper was torn from the box, then the duct tape. We heard the box being torn open, and 'bloody' packages being removed one by one. The animal came last. Silence as the animal 'cage' was slowly opened. Not knowing what to expect. Was it dead? Was it alive? Being careful as possible so the new pet didn't escape. More silence as he read the instruction sheet, then slowly freed the animal from its confinement with just a few tell tale raspberry seeds on its face. Then # $ % & * X # # # # !!!!!

You sent me a PET ROCK! All of this because of a PET ROCK!

We quickly sang a verse of "We Wish You a Merry Christmas!" and wished him a happy new year with his pet! Then hung up, sides bursting from laughter.

Seriously speaking, a rock can be a very good friend. The psalmist often referred to God as a 'rock', a 'cornerstone'. (Ps. 18:2; Ps. 18:31; Ps. 28:1; Ps 71:3; Ps. 61:2, and 62:6.) In church we sing the old familiar tune, "Rock of Ages". The children sing "Jesus is the Rock", "I Go to The Rock", and "His Banner Over Me is Love". Sitting on my desk next to me now is a large, smooth, polished and varnished rock painted with the words, 'Jesus is my rock and my salvation'. Know anyone who needs the Rock for Christmas????

THE CHINA CABINET

As I slowly sip my tea, glad to be indoors, I observe the winter storm raging outside my patio door. The snow is already two feet deep with plummeting temperatures and howling winds that promise to continue on through the night. Yet, in its fierceness, there is beauty. My eyes now drift to the small Amish made china cabinet that sits to the left of the patio door. I like its fine plain lines and finish that do not detract from the beauty of its golden oak or what it holds within.

Originally, the cabinet held my mother's set of cherry blossom dishes; however, surrounded by the boldness of Christmas, the fragile blossoms seemed out of place. Therefore, they were carefully tucked away for the holidays and in their place, I gathered odds and ends from among my Christmas things that reflected the holiday season: a Christmas teapot that I seldom used, one Lenox dish with a cardinal on a branch of holly, a white spool angel, a glittery green Christmas tree; and so it went until I had filled the cabinet with odds and ends that surprisingly melded together in a display of Christmas cheer.

Now Christmas has passed. The holiday things have been put away for another year, and the blustery storm without has left me even less in the mood for cherry blossoms than before. But what to do? In contrast to the bright colors of Christmas, I decide on white: winter white, to match the storm without. The search begins throughout the house. What do I have that is white and appropriate for a china cabinet? A plain white cup and saucer with the word, 'Mother' written in gold. It had belonged to my grandmother and was about a hundred years old. All this time, it had just been stored in the bottom of the china cabinet. Now it took center place on the top shelf.

In a closet, I find a Bavarian crystal vase, a reminder of my time in the Czech Republic. Under the cabinet lights, it appears to be made of ice. Ice! That reminds me of the cut glass pitcher given me as a farewell gift from my students when I moved to another state. Now I need something large for the bottom shelf, but what? I search the house for WHITE, anything white, and discover a large white soup tureen, a gift from a friend who had recently died.

Two plain white dishes, left over from the church rummage sale serve as back drops. I take my plain white sugar and creamer set from the table and place them in the cabinet. I need white! White! I am desperate for white: anything white! I can use the white spool angel from Christmas. I have a spring of pine with white snow flocking, a white magnolia, three white porcelain trees, and two tiny antique white birds. One thing more is needed. But what? And then it hits me, the lighted white glass church from our Great Room. The Great Room will have to do without! Finished, I stand back and observe the result.

I think back to when I was serving in the mission field in the Czech Republic. I was surprised that the china cabinets I saw there did not contain sets of matching dishes (like my cherry blossoms). Instead, they held an eclectic collection of items given by a variety of relatives and friends. Hence, each item was different and each had a memory of the person who had given it.

I now stand back to observe my cabinet, my winter white cabinet, and reflect on the items within that most likely would not have made it to display except for my need for white. Each item brings a memory, and there in the center is the church, reminding us that

Christ, through His work of redemption, makes US white as the snow.

> *"Purge me with hyssop, and I shall be clean;*
> *Wash me, and I shall be whiter than snow."* Ps. 51: 7

4

THINGS I THOUGHT I'D NEVER DO

"If we are ever in doubt what to do, it is a good rule to ask ourselves what we shall wish on the morrow that we had done.
- Lord Avebury, John Lubbock

GOD AND THE ORGANIST

Do you believe that God talks to people? I do. Not in the sense that Joan Rivers might ask, "Can we talk?", but very subtly like an unrelenting thought that just won't let go. A few years back, God put it on my heart to get a piano. What's so strange about that you might ask. Well, for one thing, I didn't know how to play the piano. When I was in seventh grade, my grandfather died and I inherited his accordion. Years later, teaching in the middle grades, I would occasionally bring it out and my students would ask, "What's that?" Yes, I was an accordion player, not especially good, but it got me by; and it was much more portable than a piano. The old accordion accompanied me to camps, schools, hospitals, VBS's, Christmas caroling, outdoor services, and occasionally an indoor church service; but other than the right hand keyboard, it was nothing like a piano!

Then one December, I became obsessed with the idea of a piano. I had to have a piano! I searched for piano sales. I looked for used pianos. I checked them out in music stores. I read up on pianos. Piano possession became a burning desire, but no matter how I looked at it, I couldn't afford a piano. Then the idea struck. Christmas wasn't far afar. When my husband asked what a wanted for Christmas, I said, "A piano!".

He laughed and asked, "Why do you want a piano?"

"I don't know," I dumbly replied. "I just have to have a piano."

"We can't afford a piano," was his reply.

"I know," I said. "But I found the perfect one on sale, and I don't want anything else; not even so much as a candy cane. If you and our kids (already grown) chip in together and just put the down payment on a piano, I believe I can make the monthly payments on it (probably for the rest of my life was my thinking). Well, Christmas came with lots of little gifts but no piano. For the life of me, I couldn't understand why I wanted a piano so badly anyway, but I did. Then two days after Christmas, the doorbell rang and in rolled a brand new Story and Clark walnut cased piano with the biggest red bow I had ever seen. Not only had my husband purchased the piano for me, but he volunteered to make all the payments on it until it was paid off with the understanding that I would never get another present for any occasion until the piano was paid off. And that probably meant not for next Christmas either!

As I stood admiring this beautiful piece of craftsmanship, tears filled my eyes and a peace seemed to fill my soul. Slowly, I lifted the covering and gingerly touched one of the keys and was rewarded with one of the most beautiful sounds I have ever heard. Then, stepping back and looking again through different eyes at this beautiful instrument, the color seemed to drain from my face.

"What's the matter?" my husband asked. "Isn't it the one you wanted?"

"Yes, it's perfect," I replied.

"Then what's wrong?"

"I don't know how to play the piano. (DUH!) What am I supposed to do with this?"

"I don't know," he said, " but it's what you wanted, and now you have it!"

Well, the only logical thing left to do was for me to take piano lessons. My accordion background allowed me to begin at the early intermediate piano level, but it wasn't easy. The right hand was a breeze, but the left hand was a nightmare. There were no buttons to push and no bellows to squeeze. And whoever decided it would be a good idea to read the notes in the left hand differently than the right? ! Developing the left hand coordination, getting a feel for where the correct keys were without looking down at the keyboard, and then pausing while my brain figured out which note was being represented in the left hand was (and still is) a challenge to this 'mature' brain. To add to the 'brain switch', I could no longer tap my right foot for rhythm, but had to work pedals instead. I struggled to painfully learn each song. I am sure my husband regretted ever buying the piano on more than one occasion. After six months of lessons, I was called into the mission field (but that is another story). Returning, I continued to practice daily since that is all that could help me at the point I had reached. I knew what to do. It was the doing that was the challenge.

Then it started. Innocently enough at first, or so it seemed. Our organist asked me to play the electronic piano in church JUST DURING THE OFFERING one day as a variety to the organ that she played in the balcony. That one day turned into once a month during the offering, and so it went until the day came when she would be out of town and wouldn't be there for Sunday service. You guessed it. I played the entire service, but only with songs that I selected and knew how to play (they were hymns but not necessarily in our 1941 red hymnal).

As time went on, for a variety of reasons, our organist was no longer able to handle all our church services. A procession of part time organists followed but always left after a short time also for a variety of reasons: moving, health, back to college, etc. Organists are hard to find in our area, especially for the pay our small church is able to afford. I started playing the electronic piano for more services and 'rewriting' some of the left hand to make it easier for me to play at a good singing tempo.

Then it happened! The electronic piano died. Our organist would have 'none of it'.

"Jill," she said, "get up there and play that organ!"

"Whoa, there just a minute," I said. "You have forgotten that I am an ACCORDION player who struggles through church services on the piano. There is no way that I can or will learn to play that organ. Two handed playing is about all I can handle now without having two keyboards, a bunch of 'tabs and knobs' that I know nothing about, pedals, and that keyboard thing you play with your feet! I don't even know how to turn the thing on!

With frustration on her face and determination in her voice that I had never heard until this point, she said, "Get up there! Choose a keyboard and just play like you would play a piano! I will show you how to turn it on!"

To make a long story short, for better or for worse, I now play the organ for two services a month. We have an agreement: I will not take organ lessons (too costly and too much for this brain I think), the church will not pay me, and NO ONE WILL COMPLAIN about my playing. I am still a nervous wreck on the Sundays I play, but very slowly, emphasis on 'very slowly' I am improving a little bit at a time. I am not gifted in this area, but I am, reluctantly and against my will, becoming attached to the organ and have begun experimenting with those little tabby things. I mentioned to our organist that I was considering taking just a 'few' organ lessons to better understand the instrument and what it can do. She said that I needn't do that and has agreed to meet with me one day to explain the tabs (or whatever they are called).

Last Sunday, as I lined up my music (I never realized that an organist plays a minimum of SEVEN SONGS in each service!) I asked myself, 'How did I ever come to this?' , and thought back to the time when I 'needed' a piano. That was where it all started! God is all knowing and sees the future. *Lord, You know all things.* (John 21:17) Could it just be that God foresaw this need in our church nine years ago and put the piano obsession in my mind? Could that planted seed be what lead me to what I now do? If so, what else may be in store for this accordion player without much talent but a love for music? I shudder to think. That being the case, I wonder why He didn't choose someone with more talent. Nevertheless, I firmly believe that God speaks to us, sometimes for reasons we don't know or understand; and that He sometimes uses other people to help bring about His will. I must add that playing my piano at home is a blessing to me. It's been several years now since I have played my accordion. But in conclusion, I must warn you. Beware of an organist who begins by saying; "Just play one little song during the offering for me." Organists can be very sneaky people!

FOOD FOR THE BODY AND SOUL

People often pray asking God to give them direction in their lives. But how do you know for sure what God's will is in any given situation. I learned that God's will is evident in His provision. He guides and provides.

When my husband sensed God's call into the Christian ministry in mid-life, our family was faced with a financial crisis. We would be down to one paycheck and there was no doubt that our level of personal comfort and quality of life would be affected. We had two teenagers at home, the same mortgage payment, the same car payments, and we all needed to eat. In addition, we were faced with seminary fees for courses, books, computer and other necessities. I knew my husband had felt that tug to attend seminary for some time, but I needed to know that this was God's will and not just wishful thinking on his part.

My husband passed the first hurdle and was accepted into the seminary program. Then the financial challenges began at home. We examined the household bills and decided to cash in a life insurance policy. We cancelled our cable television subscription and were now down to one station. We also cancelled the newspaper and decided to check out the nearly new shops for clothing items instead of buying new. A steak at mealtime meant it was in the form of hamburger. Those were difficult times.

The Lord did not desert us. The help started coming through God's people. Both the church we attended and the church regional district came up with money to pay for some of the courses. An uncle suddenly passed away and left my husband $5,000 in his will. That paid for the computer and books. My parents provided housing for their son-in-law as their home was a convenient distance from the seminary. Another student shared gas and parking costs. We would suddenly get an envelope in our mailbox at home containing fifty dollars or a gift certificate towards the cost of food. So many people remembered us in practical ways that I just knew God was in it.

At Thanksgiving and Christmas the church would collect food for the food bank in our town and always included our family in these blessings. We had a pantry full of canned goods, cereals, potatoes, and other groceries. One day our daughter decided to organize the pantry into categories, and she discovered that we had been given 22 boxes of Kraft dinner. We stared at the shelves in amazement. Twenty-two boxes! Then we burst out laughing. I had become an expert at creating gourmet Kraft dinner, adding meat, vegetables, and spices to re-create the ordinary into a palate delight.

We lived two years this way under God's grace and blessing. Then my husband began a vicarage earning half salary. We had used up all our savings, and God had provided the rest. We ended up with no debt. It was an amazing time, and a time I shall always remember. God says in His Word,

> "Therefore I say to you, 'Do not worry about your life, what you will; nor about the body, what you will put on.. . . For all these things the nations of the world seek after, and your Father knows that you need these things. But seek the kingdom of God, and all these things shall be added to you." (Luke 12:22,30-31)

Trusting the Lord is how to know Him. To know Him is to love Him. To love Him creates the desire to serve Him. To serve Him we must trust Him. It's the only way.

THE FEET OF HIS SAINTS (I SAM. 2:9)

When I was a little girl, the thing I loved the best was to hear my mother recount anecdotes about family events. Some were amusing, others tragic, but they were always entertaining or inspiring. I am now a pastor's wife, and I relate especially to stories about my grandmother, who was also a pastor's wife. During the 1920s, she and my grandfather lived in the Baltic States close to the northwest border of Estonia and Russia. Most churches were imposing, heavy stone structures, and the interiors were not designed with comfort in mind.

Although my grandmother passed away many years ago, the following story lives on in our family. Grandmother was a very warm, compassionate and caring individual and greatly loved by the congregation she and my grandfather were serving. However, she had an impatient, impulsive nature that sometimes led to embarrassing or even comical situations. She suffered greatly with cold feet. In Estonia at the time, it was quite acceptable not to heat the churches during the cold winter months. My grandfather took his calling as a servant of God very seriously and would preach long sermons, often lasting two hours. The farm folk who came to church in their sleighs were prepared for this and quite happy to listen for so long. However, my grandmother would be freezing during the service and could hardly wait until it was over. She would signal grandfather with her eyes as he was preaching. Sometimes he wouldn't notice or more likely pretend not to notice, and the sermon would continue unabated. Then she would mumble, "O my goodness, O my goodness!" as her feet got colder and more numb.

One Sunday, the sermon seemed to drag on longer than usual and her icy feet became almost intolerable. Grandfather had ignored absolutely every wink, raised eyebrow or other signal she could manage. Impulsively she leapt to her feet, and shouted in a strong, clear voice, "Fritz! Amen!" There was a hush. Grandfather's face was frozen in shock. She was immediately overcome with embarrassment and sat down, but the damage was done. The congregation immediately forgave her this little indiscretion because they loved her; in fact, they all saw it as rather funny. My grandfather didn't handle it quite so graciously.

As a pastor's wife myself, I appreciate this little story. I've tried using my own special signals when I have thought that my husband's sermon had tested our ability to sit in those hard wooden pews. Maybe using modern technology would be kind of fun. Give him a Blackberry for Christmas and send him a text message during the sermon, "Hey, Honey! Amen!" This flight of fancy will likely get me no results either. So I'll just stick to something more discreet - tapping my watch.

5

WHEN THINGS GO WRONG

"The greatest discovery of my generation is that human beings can alter their lives by altering their attitudes of mind."

-William James

LOOK FOR THE LIGHT

Ever have one of those days when everything you try seems to go wrong? A day when everyone and everything in the universe seems to conspire against you, and you find yourself asking, "Why me?" Little did I know when I woke up that morning that I was about to encounter one such day. I am the creative worship director at our church, and on the night before that fateful service, I had decided to try something new for church the next day. (In retrospect, probably not a good idea on short notice.)

Some years ago at another church, my husband who plays the guitar and I who play the accordion, along with someone who played the tambourine, performed "The Lord's Prayer" in church. Despite what you might think, it was quite lovely, very reverent, and was well received. Since the readings for the next day dealt with the Lord's Prayer and I direct the choir, the plan on this day was to have the choir sing with this new accompaniment. I didn't think there would be any difficulty in learning it in an hour before church because ours is a unison choir and the melody would be familiar. I couldn't have been farther from the truth.

First, I went over the song with the choir several times until they seemed comfortable with the words and melody. Check! Next, I got someone to volunteer to play the tambourine. Check! After that, we had to get the instruments in tune. Check! Then my husband had to practice a bit to remember the chords. Check! Lastly, we put it all together. Disaster! My husband leaned in close with his electric guitar to see the music. When he did this, he drowned out my accordion making it impossible for me to hear what I was playing. The result was disaster. If he moved further away, he couldn't see the music. With a half hour until church, there was no time to copy music, set up another stand, or experiment with standing arrangements keeping in mind that I needed room to extend my bellows. I decided to put this idea on the back burner for another day when there would be more time to 'work out the bugs'.

Idea one: Shot down!

No problem, I hurriedly got ready for the rest of what was planned for this day. I highlighted the morning bulletin for activities for which I needed to be ready. I set up my music on the organ in the balcony. I set up my music on the electronic keyboard on the main floor. I set up puppet equipment in the sacristy. I went over the script with my puppet assistant in the balcony. I checked with my husband for the place in the service where he would say the 'lead in' for the puppet, and lastly, I chose a different song for the choir to sing.

I played the prelude and first hymn on the organ. All went well until an ominous sound began to rise near the lectern. It was barely audible, but gradually grew louder and louder for all to hear. About the time I figured out what it was, my husband paused and asked the congregation, "What is that sound?! It sounds like a washing machine?" Hearing no response, I moved to the mike and announced from the balcony, "That would be the electronic piano." I 'll be right down." My husband would be leading a new song today, and I wanted to accompany him on the electronic piano which would be closer to him than the organ. (He is a wonderful singer but tends to create his own melodies without accompaniment.) **Idea two: Shot down!**

He decided to charge forward and sing it acapella - a bad decision. I joined in, directing the congregation like a choir, and we made it through with a few laughs. I made a hasty retreat back to the balcony to be ready for the next song when the time came. Time for song two on the organ. I flipped on the switch, started to play, and somewhere there was a sticking note drowning out the song. (Vincent Price would have loved it!) Trying unsuccessfully to 'unstick' the note, whatever it might be, I turned off the organ. **Idea three. Shot down!** I rushed downstairs, and again lead the congregation in singing the song acapella, and hurried back to the balcony. I was beginning to feel like a jack-in-box, and hoped I appear as crazy as I was beginning to feel.

Unable to fix the organ or the electronic piano (the accordion was out of the question at this point), the rest of the songs were done acapella. Music out of the way, in a last attempt to save the day; at the appointed time, I again went downstairs and this time, slipped into the sacristy to prepare for the puppet portion of the service. I do a Japanese form of puppetry which involves dressing in black, pretty much like a ninja. My puppets are full figured 'vents'. I slipped on the black glove and hood, picked up my vent and waited in the 'wings' for my husband to give the lead in. And waited. And waited. And waited. Time passed and I was beginning to get pretty warm. When he finished his sermon and handed the offering plates to the ushers, I knew he had forgotten the puppet. **Strike four!**

With perspiration running down my cheek, I got the attention of the acolyte and asked him to inform the pastor that I was waiting in the wings. A whisper in his ear, and after the day we had had so far, my husband knew he was in trouble! He made the necessary adjustment, and my puppet entered. Remember the readings for the day concerned the Lord's Prayer? Well, the puppet was to begin the Lord's Prayer and God (in the balcony) would question him about what he was saying. We would end on a good note. The puppet began, but there was no 'God' to respond in the balcony. **Strike five** (Did I mention that we had visitors in the church that day?).

When the minister forgot to give the lead in for the puppet at the correct time, my balcony counterpart assumed we were going to skip the puppet routine and went to get a drink. I began the routine and when there was no response from the balcony, I improvised the part of God as well. At that moment, William, hearing the puppet, rushed upstairs and began reading his part from the beginning (the sections I had just covered). The only thing that worked correctly on that day for me was the last minute of a puppet routine which just happened to be one of the best routines I have! I was unhappy, flustered, hot, dripping wet, and I admit, somewhat angry at the world! I turned to check if the mobile over the advent wreathe was still hanging, half expecting it to have fallen into the candles and caught fire. (That had happened once before on another day). The mobile seemed to be the only thing 'hanging straight' on this day.

Frustrated and disappointed that nothing seemed to have gone right for the day, despite all my efforts; I put the puppet away and started back to the balcony at the close of a service I would like to forever forget. On my way to the balcony, Chuck stopped to talk to me, but all I could do was to mutter about how even the smallest little thing just go right on this day!!!! Grumble, grumble, grumble! Finally, after about four attempts, Chuck was able to say, "The four little children visiting the church with their parents today were a little restless, but they were motionless and never took their eyes off the puppet. I think you got through to them." And then he walked away. Shame flooded over me like an ill fitting dress. I was so concerned about 'details' that I lost sight of the purpose of what I was doing: to give praise to God. **Was I strike six?** Hopefully not.

The next week, I apologized to Chuck and thanked him for his comment. That experience has taught me that little details shouldn't keep us from praising God first and to always 'look for the light in the darkness'. That attitude could not be more demonstrated than by my friend Nettie arriving for choir the 'week after'. Seeing me, she gave a big smile and asked, "Hey, last week in church was the most fun that I've had in a long time; can we do it again this week?" "It's always a possibility," I quipped back, "if we are lucky!."

"Rejoice in the Lord always. Again I will say, rejoice!" Let your gentleness be known to all men. The Lord is at hand. Be anxious

for nothing, but in everything by prayer and supplication, with thanksgiving, let your requests be made known to God; and the peace of God, which surpasses all understanding, will guard your hearts and minds through Christ Jesus." (Phil. 4:4 -6)

ANGELS ON OVERTIME

December 23! The last day of school before Christmas break. My car was packed, and I planned on driving home as soon as school let out. This was my first year of teaching. Who would have ever believed that someday I would leave my home in Southern New Jersey and drive alone to a big city like Detroit, Michigan. Not me, that's for sure! The last four months had been a period of personal growth far beyond any expectations. I loved teaching and each of my forty-two fourth grade students, and I was anxious to tell my family and fiancé all about it.

As I neared the street I would turn on to reach my school, I noticed a car pull quickly out of a side street and cross four traffic lanes. At that point, it slid on some black ice hurling it into a car two spaces ahead of me. This was Detroit, and traffic was moving quickly. In the next few seconds, I slowed as much as possible and anticipated my next move. As expected, the car immediately in front of me rear ended the car that was hit. How could I avoid being the fourth car in the pile up? If I pulled to the right, I would end up on a city sidewalk already filled with pedestrians. If I turned to the left, I would hit the cars traveling in the lanes to the left of me. Slowing as much as possible, I had no choice but to hit the car immediately in front of me followed by a crash behind, as the next car in our lane became the fifth car in the pile up as it crashed into me. Each of us received a ticket for hitting the car in front, an accident all caused by one driver in too much of a hurry, sliding on ice!

Upon reaching my school, I told my principal what had happened. Except for a broken head and rear light and a banged up fender, the car was ok. to drive. Mr. Bierlien offered to take it to be repaired while I taught, and by the end of the day I would be able to drive to New Jersey as planned. On hearing of my reason for being late for school, my students were taking up a collection for me from their lunch money to get my car fixed. Fourth graders are the best!

3:30 p.m. finally arrived, but due to the day's unexpected beginning, followed by a day of 42 kids anxious for school to be out, and the excitement of the class Christmas party; I found myself too weary to set off on a long distance drive without some rest. **Plan B:** I decided to go back to my apartment, get some sleep, and leave around 1:00 a.m. when traffic would be less.

I set out as planned and was well into Ohio listening to Handel's "Messiah" on the radio as I drove. Few cars were traveling at that time in the morning, and I would be home in plenty of time for the Christmas Eve midnight service. Singing along with the "Hallelujah Chorus", I glanced at the hamster cage sitting on the seat next to me. It appeared as though the cage door had swung open. I reached to close it before Pete and Gladys got out, and ended up swerving to the left across four lanes where my car hit a light pole and ricocheted back again to the right shoulder, plunging down an embankment, and into a concrete culvert at fifty miles an hour. I closed the cage door and tried to start the car again. (DUH!) The back windshield was nearly pressed against the front seat and the front of the car had folded like an accordion. The doors open. It was dark, and I was alone.

After thinking for a moment, I decided to climb out the window and try to find a service station. I grabbed my purse and placed my girl scout knife in my mouth (for safety in the night- Yeah right!), freeing my hands to maneuver my body out of my newly repaired , and now squashed car. As I began my assent, I was surprised to see a large vehicle illuminated in bright lights at the top of the embankment. It was a snowplow. The driver had seen my wild drive to and fro across four lanes of highway.

"You O.K.?" he asked.

"I guess so," I replied.

"Did you fall asleep driving?" he queried.

"No, I thought my hamsters got out of the cage," I answered feeling rather foolish.

"You hurt anywhere?"

"I don't think so," I said. "My ribs just feel sore. I hit the steering wheel."

"How about the hamsters?"

"They're fine," I said blushing with embarrassment.

"I had better call an ambulance to have you checked out."

He tried to make small talk as we waited for the ambulance to arrive, but I'm afraid I wasn't a very good conversationalist after the day and now morning that I had had.

I thanked the snowplow man for his help and rode away in an ambulance to a hospital. An examination and x rays revealed that I had bruised ribs but was otherwise O.K. The only thing left for me to do, was to call my roommate back in Detroit. She had to teach a half day on the (now Dec. 24th), but came to get me once school was dismissed I waited until she met me at Elyria Memorial Hospital. We stopped at the station where my car had been towed, and I took out the hamsters, luggage, and Christmas presents. The car was totaled, but the hamsters were fine! The only thing that could be done was to try to sell the car for parts. The station man agreed to do that. He would deduct the cost of storing the car when he found a buyer. Deal.

Back again to Detroit, Michigan and our apartment. Now what? **Plan C:** I would see if I could get a flight back home at the last minute on Christmas Eve. I was in luck. I called my fiancé and my mother to tell them of my change in plans. I would be arriving in New York City and then would catch a bus to Hackensack, NJ where my fiancé would meet me.

I found someone to take care of the hamsters and just had time enough to squeeze presents into a suitcase and to get a taxi to the airport. It was snowing really hard - a white Christmas for sure. Traffic was slowed due to almost total white out conditions by the time I reached the airport. I had missed my flight! **Plan D:** Get the next flight that was leaving. No time to call my fiancé who would be waiting by the phone for my call.

Once on the plane, I became aware of how sore my ribs were every time the plane lurched. It lurched a lot! Once in the air, in addition to blizzard conditions, we encountered a thunderstorm and lightning. Such excitement! I might have been afraid except for the experiences and lack of sleep for the last two days which put me in a sort of 'coma'. People were vomiting in 'barfy' bags, and the stewardesses were skipping up and down the aisles ringing bells and singing Christmas Carols to try to calm the people. I thought it rather funny, but it hurt to laugh. I could not have been more calm than if I were dead! It seemed as though this was some comedy I was watching on TV, or at least until the plane made another lurch and woke up my ribs!

Arrival in NYC: Many of the airports had been closed by this time, and our plane circled for another two hours waiting until they could clear the runway of snow enough for a safe landing. Moving more like a zombie, I gathered my luggage and set off to find a taxi. As I neared the platform, one pulled up in front of me, and I got in.

"You are lucky to find a taxi," he announced. "Most taxis have stopped running due to white out conditions. After I drop you off at the bus station, I'm quitting for the night too."

I could barely see anything out of the car window. The snow was coming down harder than I had ever seen. I could barely make out buildings. It was New York City, and everything was still: no people, no vehicles except for my taxi on the road, no lights. NYC was in black out. It was one of the worse winter storms the city had ever experienced. Safely deposited at Port Authority, I headed for a bus to Hackensack. I was a robot moving through the crowds. I got in line and took a seat on the bus: the last seat on the last bus to leave that night. It would be several days before the city would be up and running again. Once I arrived in Hackensack, I informed my fiancé of my arrival. He had been sleeping on the floor next to the phone all night. It seems the plane that I missed had crashed, and he was beside himself with worry waiting for more information! It was now early Christmas morning. All was peaceful, and the newly fallen snow glistened in the sunlight. In two days time, God had protected me from two car crashes, one air plane crash, and from being stranded in NYC for three to four days, alone with bruised ribs and no sleep or place to go. He had provided my principal, a snowplow person, my roommate, a service station man, a taxi driver, a bus driver, and my fiancé to assist me in my journey (and don't forget the offerings of my fourth grade students!) Like the angels on that first Christmas so long ago, God had provided many angels to look after me and protect me on that memorable Christmas.

Some years later, I was once more driving on the Ohio turnpike. I searched for the concrete culvert that I had crashed into. In the entire length of the pike, there was just one culvert that I could find, and it was immediately across the four lanes from a light post for which I had to pay to have it replaced! It was located near the exit for Elyria. My husband and I had accepted teaching calls in Ohio and would be moving in the area . Over the thirty years we have lived and worked in Elyria, I have often made many visits to that same Elyria Memorial Hospital. How strange is that?! God does indeed work in mysterious ways, and I am living proof that in the words of the psalmist, *"He shall give His angels charge over you, to keep you in all your ways." (Psalm 91: 11)*. They certainly worked overtime near Christmas for me many years ago!

FOR BETTER AND FOR WORSE TIL DEATH DO US PART

And the Lord God said, "It is not good that man should be alone; I will make him a helper comparable to him." Genesis 2:18:

Today is cloudy and rainy which is so different from yesterday's bright sunshine. Yes, spring is here, and love is in the air. It's wedding season once again, and the brides and grooms are anxiously looking forward to their special day. So it was for the couple joined last evening in what was planned to be the perfect wedding. It was obvious that Tom and Elaine had eagerly planned what was to be their perfect wedding for months with great anticipation.

The bridal party included eight bridesmaids and eight groomsmen all dressed in their proper wedding attire along with a flower girl and a ring bearer who were dressed as miniature replicas of the bride and groom. My job was to be the esthetic advisor for the wedding. The wedding was not a regular church wedding, it was in a beautiful reception hall off from a restaurant/brewery. The hall was adorned with big beautiful arched windows which gave a gorgeous view of the river at sunset. Their day had finally arrived and the hall was decorated with beautiful flowers, pink ribbon bows, table clothes, and candles. The long awaited day had arrived, and it was finally time for the ceremony to begin. It was my job to give my husband the nod when everyone was lined up in the proper order, and he in turn would give the Disc Jockey a nod to begin the music.

Just before the line up began all eight bridesmaids, the bride, and the little flower girl decided that they needed to use the restroom. Thus, the ceremony started fifteen minutes later than planned by the time everyone was finally back in line. The bride's twelve year old nephews had been selected to pull the beautiful white runner down the center of the aisle, however in so doing, it tangled up a few times along the long aisle, and some of the guests helped them straighten it out so they could get it down to the altar area. Finally, music began *Pachelbel's Canon in D major*, and I reminded each bridesmaid when to begin their descent down the massive and curved stairway from the loft above. My biggest fear was that the three and a half inch heeled sandals they had chosen to match their beautiful gowns could be hazardous in their decent. I cautioned each to walk slowly to the rhythm of the music and to be careful not to fall. To my relief, each and every one of them made it to the front altar with no problem.

The ceremony had begun with no hitches until there was a loud clunk as one of the groomsmen fell to the floor in a dead faint. The ceremony momentarily stopped, and those around him jumped to aid him. Someone from below was motioning for me to get him a drink so I quickly ran through the upper loft and found a waiter setting up for another wedding reception, and asked him if he would get me a glass of water for the ailing groomsman. I waited in what seemed like an eternity for him to return with a large glass of water. After assessing my location in the top loft, I asked him if he would mind descending the stairway to deliver that special glass of water. He hesitated for a moment while I persuaded him that it really needed to get down to the ailing groomsman as fast as possible. By the time he got down with the glass of water, another groomsman went down, and a third was swaying. I stood in that loft praying and holding my breath with only a portion of the groomsmen left standing.

The ceremony continued, the vows were being stated when all of a sudden, the lights and the microphones went out. There was a major power failure, and absolutely no back up electricity to power the microphones. Now what? The ceremony continued without sound amplification and music, and then it was time to light the unity candle. As that part of the ceremony began, the Christ candle accidentally blew out, and a guest again came to the rescue with his cigarette lighter. I breathed a sigh of relief when the unity candle finally was lit. As the bride began her turn to go back to the altar, the veil fell off her head. She stood stunned for a second with it in her hands, and then walked over and handed it to her mother who was sitting in the front row. Both the bride and groom gifted their mothers with a red rose and exchanged kisses. At that moment the ring bearer and the flower girl together decided they needed their bridesmaid mothers and went up and tenaciously clung each to their respective mother's leg.

The carefully planned ceremony was finally over, and the wedding party came back down the aisle in silence with no music. I, the esthetic director, stood up in the loft looking down from above not knowing whether to laugh or to cry. How could this comedy of errors be, I asked myself? Well, to say the least I am told that they did state in their vows, for better and for worse, until death do us part. I only know for sure that life has to get better for them for what *"God has joined together let no one (or situation) separate!" Mark 10:5.*

HARD WAY LESSON

"When pride comes, then comes shame; But with the humble is wisdom."Proverbs 11:2

Have you ever been in a position of having to participate in a social that you look forward to and dread at the same time? Well, as a pastor's wife, I have to be honest and admit this has happened to me on more than one occasion. This Friday was the night when one of those occasions took place. Yes, my husband and I had been invited by a prestigious couple in our church to an event at the Aksarben Hall in Omaha, Nebraska. Now, for those of you who haven't realized it yet, Aksarben is Nebraska spelled in reverse. These special events were always expensive, so my husband and I attended very few of them, because it was impossible for us to fit them into our tight budget, but tonight was different.

This was a concert everyone had long awaited, and our impressive friends were picking us up at 7:00 P.M. sharp so that we could get there in time to get good seats. I had thought all day long about what I should wear to this event, and finally decided on my dark blue pant suit that was relatively new, and the shoes and purse I had purchased to match. Yes, I thought wearing a pantsuit that evening would not only be dressy, but warm. You see, winter days in Omaha could be both windy and cold.

I fed the children early and got ready while my husband picked up the babysitter for the evening. Promptly at 7:00 P.M. our prestigious members picked us up, and we were off to a wonderful evening of entertainment. I felt good about the evening because we had looked forward to it for quite awhile. As we neared Aksarben, we could see the beautiful bright lights which lit up the area for what seemed like miles. Finally we arrived, and got out of the car. As the four of began to walk towards the building, I felt something strange around my ankles. I wondered what was causing the problem, so I looked down at my feet only to be horrified.

There at the cuff of my slacks, was a pair of panty hose trailing behind me. I stopped dead in my tracks, not knowing exactly what to do. I could feel my face growing hotter and hotter, which I knew meant that it was probably beet red. At that moment all I could do was reach down and pull out the trailing panty hose from around my ankles and stick them in my purse. I managed to give an embarrassing laugh as everyone in our group witnessed this horrible moment in my life unfold. It seems as though I somehow had slipped my slacks and pantyhose off at the same time at my previous wearing of that suit. I had completely forgotten to remove the panty hose from the leg of my slacks when I hung them up in my closet, and the rest is history.

To say the least, my evening was ruined because all I could do was sit there and replay that horrific event over and over in my mind. However, the hard lesson I learned that night was to never double task when removing my slacks and panty hose; I would from thence forth, remove them one at a time. And, guess what? This has never, never happened to me again.

A VACATION TO REMEMBER

We left the house on a beautiful July morning eager for what was to come in the next two weeks. Yes, my husband was finally able to manage a well earned vacation. The services were planned, and the visiting preachers were lined up. The kids could hardly believe that we were headed to the Minnesota lake we'd all grown to love over the years. This year we even took our dog with us, so we were all truly together under the roof of our Yellow Ford Pinto. We had no clue of the events that were to take place as we drove and drove from our Omaha home for what seemed like an eternity to our children. After the car games, they'd always manage to ask, Are we there yet. Yes, finally their dad and I were able to say, "We have twenty five more miles left and we'll be there."

As usual we drove the long dirt road to the lake and found the cottage we had rented for the two weeks we were to be there. The cottage always needed to be big enough to accommodate our closest relatives: my mother, my sister and her family, aunts, uncles, and cousins. Yes, the reunion of the family was always a fun time for all. These were special vacations, because we were also able to visit with aunts, uncles, and cousins whom we saw only during our vacations at the lake. We had a great time with only a few hitches such as the morning when Katie and James were going fishing, and little Katie accidentally dropped her fish hook baited with a piece of ham on the floor.

Our chocolate poodle that always was anxiously waiting for a hand out was there to immediately wolf it down. Katie was devastated and in tears as we drove through the country to find a small animal veterinarian in that rural area of Minnesota. After taking X rays on our puppy's tummy which clearly revealed the fish hook, the doctor decided he would need to remove it surgically. The surgery was successful, and we spent the next several days traveling back and forth to visit our precious dog that was 'hooked up' with IV's. Finally, the day came when we could pick him up and head home. Other than having Coco on a special liquid diet, the trip home was uneventful, and we all were over joyed that he was alive and well.

When we finally reached our drive way and parked the Pinto, Katie and James jumped out of the car and ran into the garage only to stop dead in their tracks and gasp. As my husband and I got out of the Pinto we also gasped. There was a strong and unusual stench in the air which none of us had previously ever encountered. What was that smell?! Well, as we all perused the garage hunting for the cause of the stench, my husband lifted the lid to our freezer, and we immediately located that mysterious odor. It was strawberries that my husband had volunteered to preserve in our freezer during the summer months for our kids' school.

We had been gone long enough to have missed the bad storm that had come through knocking out the electricity which in turn caused our fuse box to die. The stench in the air had a tinge of strawberry odor; however it was obvious to my husband that the melted strawberries had been fermenting for two weeks in our freezer. In fact, the fermentation process was so powerful, that it had actually caused the inside paint of the freezer to bubble. Now we were stuck with a very poor grade of strawberry wine and a freezer that we needed to dispose of. What a welcome home! Yes, as we reminisce over that vacation we have often asked , "How many times during your life could you possibly have a vacation like the one we experienced that time when our children were still very young? !"

"The memory of the righteous is blessed." Proverbs 10:7

EASTER LILIES

As I dusted and vacuumed the house, I wondered what I'd do with my time if I weren't getting ready for my mom's visits at Christmas and Easter. I'd already baked some desserts, and planned the meals ahead of time, because I found it was so much easier to visit when the food matters were out of the way. Besides, the holidays were a much busier time for our family with the numerous activities we needed to attend and all of the special services which take place in a large church. Oh well, I thought, the children and I always enjoyed my mother's visits during the holidays. I somehow felt a bit guilty, because we could never go home during these special times of the year. Since my father's death, mom always wanted and needed to be with the family, so she came to us, rather than our going home to see her.

I had to be done with chores by three since it was my day to pick the kids up from school. I planned to take them home, give them a quick snack, and then stick a roast in the oven to be ready by seven thirty. We had to be at the airport by five, and it was a good thirty minutes from where we lived, so my timing had to be accurate. My husband arrived home near four- thirty and we all took off in the family car to meet grandma at the airport. As we waited, the kids became more and more excited, because grandma's visits were always a treat for them.

"Here we are", my husband proclaimed as his eyes scanned the parking garage for a spot to put our car. At that time it was perfectly appropriate to meet your guests at the gates when their plane arrived. We walked quickly, because the monitors stated that the St. Louis flight was arriving on time. As we arrived at the gate, the passengers were already deplaning, and we stood with our eyes fixed on the door to catch our first glimpse of her. "There she is!" our son yelled. Grandma spotted us in the crowd and began to wave. Yes, she was as excited as the children were! I will always remember how her eyes twinkled each time she saw us waiting for her. She had an exuberant smile and tremendous energy for a woman her age. In fact there were times that her energy wore me out, and I was her kid!

The next day was Saturday, and we were scheduled to take a trip over to the church to make sure everything was ready for the Easter Sunrise service. Yes, all the bulletins were in place for the ushers, the candles were fresh, the cross was decorated, and the robes had been ironed. And oh, dozens of Easter lily plants donated by various members had been carefully placed on a special stand that was used each year to decorate the church for that special morning which celebrated when Jesus rose from the dead.

The Easter lily display was a tradition in that church, and it was beautiful to say the least. My mother had never before seen such a beautiful array of Easter lilies and quickly approached the flowers to get a better look at them. Just as she stepped forward, she tripped on the foot of the stand that held what seemed like hundreds of plants, and down they all fell right on top of my poor mother. She rose quickly dusting herself off and apologizing for the calamity that she had caused. However, she and I spent the next several hours organizing and reorganizing the lily plants to the arrangement we thought had been the original scheme. Not only did we rearrange the plants, we also ended up vacuuming the remaining dirt off the sacristy's carpet.

Although the Easter lily disaster was horrifying at the time, it became a story which we all remembered and joked about until my mother's death. Now, it has become a fond memory and a reminder that Easter is not about the lilies, but rather the celebration of everlasting life which my sainted mother now enjoys. For all the Saints who from the labors rest.

"He is not here, but is risen! Luke 24:6

HAPPENSTANCES

True instances of 'Happenstance' - a chance circumstance or happening.

- The 36 straw angels on a mobile hanging over the lighted advent wreathe flew: down into the lighted candles in the middle of "Angels from the Realm of Glory".

- A fly flew into the communion cup during the Eucharist. (Did its soul go to heaven?)

- A 'biker pack' walked down the center aisle of a large formal church in the middle of the service and during a baby's baptism. (A sudden sucking in of air could be heard, but no one fainted.)

- A visiting pastor didn't know that Dan the organist in the balcony was blind. The minister announced a song with 24 verses but failed to tell the organist to only play the first four when the congregation was used to singing all the verses of a song.

- During a Wednesday night service, the minister's teen age daughter was in the car talking to her boyfriend on a wireless phone that was on the same frequency as the wireless microphone within the church. OOPS!!!!

- A bee flew into the minister's mouth while he was giving the eulogy at a grave site.

- The teenage acolyte was late for church, so the 85 year old usher lighted the altar candles with a wooden match that he struck on his zipper.

- A visitor from a Full Gospel church attended a conservative Lutheran church and began talking in tongues.

- The minister's wife was making 'romantic advances' to her husband while in his office before the start of church when his microphone was on.

- The acolyte fell asleep at the front of the church during the minister's sermon.

- The minister dropped the communion wafer down the low cut dress of a particularly buxom woman and had to retrieve it.

- A toddler escaped her mother's control and took a stroll around the altar during the pastor's sermon.

- A white dove flew in an open window and landed on the altar rail during service.

- The organ key got stuck during the reading of the Gospel.

- The pastor wore sneakers and shorts under his clerics for a quick exit after church for a Racquetball Competition.

- Buckets had to be placed on the pews during the service to catch dripping from a leaking roof.

- The altar guild forgot to fill the communion cups on communion day.

- A visiting pastor arrived to preach at the wrong church.

- The minister got his sleeve caught in the door when exiting the sacristy and someone had to get the key to unlock the door.

- Children held kittens that had been abandoned in the church parking lot in their laps during the church service.

- It was discovered that the church was out of wine on a communion Sunday, and the minister ended up going to a 'Speak EZ' to purchase wine 'illegally' on a Sunday where blue laws were in effect.

- A 'church' mouse was found shivering and starving near the pulpit. It was rescued and given water and communion wafers to eat until the end of service when a teenager took it home and cared for it until it was healthy enough to be released in the wild.

- Mary and Joseph failed to show up for the children's Christmas pageant and two adults were 'drafted' to play the parts and ad-lib their lines while wearing bathrobes for costumes.

- The church trustee entered the parsonage to do repairs and caught the minister's wife in the shower by mistake.

- The minister was issued a ticket for speeding while driving a carful of 'church ladies' home from a meeting in a neighboring town.

- Your contact in a foreign country came a day too early to pick you up from the airport, and you were left standing alone in an airport after being notified that the airlines had also lost your luggage with all of your information in it.

AND WHO SAYS CHURCH IS BORING!

6

MOUNTAIN TOP EXPERIENCES

"A Thing of Beauty is a joy forever."

-KEATS

I DIDN'T KNOW

I DIDN'T KNOW that there was a Lutheran Slovak Evangelical Lutheran Church (SELC) tucked behind a shopping mall not twenty minutes from my home and that my husband would get a call there to be its minister.

I DIDN'T KNOW that there was such a thing as an SELC district within the Lutheran Church Missouri Synod (LCMS) and that while all the other districts were geographically organized, ex. Ohio District, Atlantic District, etc., the SELC had no geographical bounds but was spread throughout the US and Canada.

I DIDN'T KNOW that shortly after my husband was installed as minister into this congregation that I would receive a letter from the LCMS mission board informing me that six people were being considered for a four month stay in the mission field in Czech Republic, and would I like to be considered as a candidate for the position.

I DIDN'T KNOW where the Czech Republic was located on a map, but with the letter still in my hands, I told my husband that I thought I would be shortly leaving for the mission field.

He asked, "How do you know that they will choose you. There are six candidates."

I said, **"I just know."**

I DIDN'T KNOW how much this news would mean to the Slovak people of our new church or how much it would bind me to my new church family.

I DIDN'T KNOW how much 'the laying on of hands' by the leaders of our church would affect me until the last elder, a senior citizen by the name of Andy, said his prayer in Slovak. Tears steaming from my eyes, I was overcome by the fact that this was not just a dream but reality, and in a few days, I would be living where everyone (but me) spoke Slovak!

I DIDN'T KNOW that my luggage would be lost with the address of the hotel where I would be staying, and that my contact in Ostrava would mistake my day of arrival and come the day before I was scheduled to arrive, and that my husband back home was now frantic as to what may have happened to me when he received a phone call asking where I was.

I DIDN'T KNOW, as I stood alone in an empty airport, what had happened to the people who were supposed to meet me and that no one over the age of 18 could speak English, and what to do next.

I DIDN'T KNOW, feeling alone and helpless, that when I feebly said the word 'TAXI', that it was the same in Slovak, and that the plainly dressed man who did not know English but escorted me to an unmarked car with a playboy bunny hanging from the rear view mirror, to a hotel apparently 40 miles away, was not a 'mass murderer', but apparently he was not or I would not be writing this today.

I DIDN'T KNOW that no one in the small hotel where I would be living spoke English.

I DIDN'T KNOW that I would be teaching alone in a rented hotel room rather than at the university.

I DIDN'T KNOW that I would not be provided with a translator as told, but that one of my students in each of the classes that I taught would have to volunteer to translate when necessary.

I DIDN'T KNOW that I would be living and serving alone in a town about 60 miles from my contact.

I DIDN'T KNOW anything about travel in Europe but ended up in a trolley or train garage more than once from missing my stop.

I DIDN'T KNOW that I could be totally immersed in a foreign culture and still be able to communicate through mime, sign, and who knows what else!

I DIDN'T KNOW that standing on a mountain top in the Tetras and looking over the scenic view below that this four month mission stay would be the life altering 'Mountain top experience' of my life. But it was!

Therefore we also pray always for you that our God would count you worthy of this calling, and fulfill all the good pleasure of His goodness and the work of faith with power, that the name of our Lord Jesus Christ may be glorified in you, and you in Him according to the grace of our God and the Lord Jesus Christ. (2 Thess. 1:11-12)

IT FEELS GOOD TO GIVE

"It will never work. People in the Czech Republic will not accept pamphlets that are being handed out on street corners. You're just wasting your time." Such was the warning of a fellow American. I was teaching college classes in the mission field, and my students had just finished making Easter cards inviting people to their church. I discussed it with my class and decided to make it more enticing by including the card in a bag of Easter goodies consisting of an Easter cookie and candies.

So far, I had been able to find everything in the Czech Republic that was available in the States: everything until now that is. There were no jelly beans! My students had no idea what a jelly bean was. I mentioned this in a letter back home. Shortly later I was surprised to receive a package from home. What could weigh so much? Jelly beans!. The postage to mail them had cost about ten times the cost of the candy; but my brother had sent them to me, and my pupils were delighted. I formed an assembly line of students with goodies to fill the bags. I watched as they talked (pop - a jelly bean disappeared into a mouth) and laughed (another jelly bean gone), and assembled the goody bags (Yum! Another one missed the bag!) They were having a blast! It was a good thing he had sent a ten pound bag! There was just enough to fill both bags and stomachs.

My American acquaintance still doubted that the bags would be accepted, so I thought of yet another idea. What if clowns delivered the treats? Being a liturgical clown, I had brought my grease paints and a few props with me. I had conducted several clown worship services, and now I would proselytize my students! They arrived early for class and painstakingly applied the paints to their faces. The liturgical clown is a mime, but students were uncomfortable working the streets alone. Therefore I sent them off in pairs on different streets with the treats and a vow of silence. We were to meet back in the classroom at an appointed time. I, in the mean time, worked alone making balloon animals for children I met. The gypsy children in particular were thrilled to receive the treats and balloon animals from a Clown for Christ.

Later, back in the classroom, all the treats had been distributed along with the Easter message; and my students sat plain faced and still as I conducted the debriefing of the experience.

What happened? What did you experience? How do you feel? Finally, as it was time for them to leave for their next class, Jarek said, "It feels good to be able to give." The response surprised me.

Yes, it does feel good to be able to give. My mother loved giving little gifts to all her grandchildren (twenty-four at the time of her death), and I copied my mother in that respect. However, I had never thought of what a blessing it was to have enough to be able to give to others. This was a double blessing: to have all you really need and enough to share; and what better gift to share than that of eternal life through Jesus Christ, our Lord!

"God loves a cheerful giver." (2 Cor. 9:7)

THE DOVE FROM HEAVEN

And John bore witness, saying, "I saw the Spirit descending from heaven like a dove, and He remained upon Him." John 1: 32 .

What a beautiful spring day! It was an exceptionally warm and sunny day in late Spring in a southwest Chicago suburb. It was Pentecost Sunday, and the choir had just finished the hymn Holy Spirit, God of Love which was one chosen especially to celebrate Pentecost. As I sat in the church balcony attired in my blue choir robe singing the hymn, I was thankful that someone had remembered to open the stain glass window behind the choir allowing a gentle breeze to cool us as we sang. Yes, the Chicago suburbs did get warm in the late spring, and I often wondered why the church fathers had built such a beautiful sanctuary without an air conditioner.

As the congregation sang the final stanza "Oh, fulfill Thy gracious Word: Bless us with Thy favor . . . Amen," I began to prepare myself for the liturgy, which was to be followed by an anthem and another hymn. The well planned service moved on through the liturgy with the Gloria Patri, the Kyrie, and the Gloria in Excelsis. Finally, it was time for the choir to lead the congregation in one of my favorite praise hymns: *Oh that I Had a Thousand Voices.*

It was obvious that the organist also loved this hymn because he turned up the volume and threw himself into making it a powerful hymn presentation. As the congregation began to sing verse four : "All creatures that have breath and motion, That throng the earth, the sea, the sky..." a beautiful dove flew into the church through the open window. The dove glided above the choir member heads, over the congregation, and landed in the front of the church on the communion rail.

At that point everything in the service stopped as people were absolutely stunned. Not only had the dove entered the church, he remained perched on the communion rail facing my husband as he presented his sermon, and on through to the very end of the service. Did the dove represent the presence of God? The stunned congregation became convinced that this incidence was no coincidence, but rather that it indeed was God reminding us of His Spiritual presence in our midst.

Since that memorable day of Pentecost, I've been told that this profound story circulated throughout the suburban Chicago churches. And yes, there is a hymn that reflects the heart of this true story: Holy Spirit, the Dove Sent from Heaven which, without a doubt proclaims the peace from God that filled each person's being in our church on that Pentecost Sunday.

7

MINISTRY STYLE

"I would have every minister of the gospel address his audience with the zeal of a friend, with the generous energy of a father, and with the exuberant affection of a mother."

- FENELON

SMALL RURAL LUTHERAN CHURCH

If you are new and just starting out in your ministry, it might be helpful for you to know a little about different styles of ministry depending on the location of the church. Although all churches and congregations have their ups and downs just like any other family, I have found that I, personally, relate best to the small rural church. I feel very isolated in large suburban congregations. Now my friend is a 'big town girl', and just the style (or lack thereof) in clothes alone would probably make her want to run far away from the rural church. My husband and I have served in three rural churches thus far, and whereas the following list may at times sound like bits from a comedy routine, I assure you that it is for real.

- There is generally at least one person called 'Bubba' or by a similar pet name. Note: 'Bubba' is not limited to just the South.
- Directing choir during hunting season is generally very frustrating due to a lack of male voices.
     The same applies for baseball season if you are directing a youth choir or have coaches in your adult choir.
- The average Sunday attendance is about 60 or less. You get more if you have a dinner after church.
- In the summer, every car in the church parking lot that isn't locked has a zucchini in the front seat. You may have heard

this before, but I assure, it is a reality. I know because I am one of those over zealous gardeners that does not like to see anything go to waste and sometimes over plant.

- Something that I have always envied is the family that has four generations all sitting in the same pew on Sundays.
- I personally love having church outside at the pavilion on hot days. Air conditioners are seldom found in small, rural churches.
- People bring salt licks and corn for the church deer, and hunting THOSE deer is forbidden.).
- It helps to be 'handy' and like working with your hands. Small churches have one minister who also shovels the snow from the church doors in the winter and tars the church roof in the summer (among a number of other things not taught at the seminary).
- Fresh vegetables, homemade blood sausage, butchered meat, and baked goods are listed as fringe benefits for the pastor
- Only the three senior citizens who can still fit into the suits they were married in wear suits to church
- If you miss one church service, you have a dozen people inquiring about your health. (Do they take attendance or what?!)
- There often is no custodian. Families take turns cleaning the church. The same goes for mowing the lawn, painting the church, and maintaining church property.
- The minister's wife often has a ministry of her own. The pastor and his wife are interviewed and 'called' as a 'team'. If you have a full time job, you are excused from attending a lot of meetings. I recommend a full time job. I personally am not a 'committee' person. I like to find something that needs to be done that no one else is doing. Some of the things I have chosen to do is to make and rotate church banners, trim the church hedges, start and direct a choir, work with creative worship, teach senior citizens, teach VBS, play the organ half time, direct a chime choir, tell Biblical stories, and run about

four money makers a year to financially support the above. One caveat: Beware of 'territory'. I have never been on the altar guild and dare not touch their 'stuff'. I also stay out of the kitchen except when organizing money makers.

- All money makers involve food or used items.
- The church organ generally has something unique and unusual about it. Its high notes may make dogs howl or it may have a habit of having a key stick in the middle of a song. Our electronic piano has a habit of sometimes sounding like a washing machine. No one can figure out why. Some have suggested that it may be possessed, but so far no one appears to have the gift of exorcism.
- There is a baseball diamond behind the church
- Music is provided by a part time organist, the minister's wife, student volunteers, and/or a boom box. Prior lessons are not a requirement.
- Any clothes bought since 1980 are considered 'in style'. Blue jeans are always in style. I have heard that camouflage outfits are considered 'the thing' in the South, but I have never served in the South to really know.
- Acolytes wear sneakers and shorts under their robes
- The minister wears sneakers and shorts under his robe when scheduled for an early racquetball match or similar activity right after church.
- Seven Bible classes and confirmation classes are offered on a weekly basis by the minister
- There are around 11 shut-ins and two confirmands.
- In farm country, addresses all begin with Rural Route____. When making visitations, if you can make it to the first farm, they can give you directions to the next home. It is best not to go at night when it is difficult to see the landmarks, e.g., green silo, Black Angus cows, soybean field, etc.
- Special fund-raisers are organized for a new septic tank, roofing materials, a furnace, new carpeting, or anything else in the line of church maintenance.
- There are openings on all committees: join the church and

become an officer!

- One accordion, a tambourine, and a guitar   constitutes a praise band.
- Multimedia equipment consists of a TV and overhead projector
- Youth group -' 5 teens
- When not in use, the organ is covered with plastic in case of rain.
- Crumbs are left for the church mouse (but only by the animal lovers who believe that God also loves vermin).
- Members are not perfect and can get pretty riled up over what color the church carpet should be, whether or not to get the tower clock fixed, or whether to update a 60 year old hymnal. CHANGE has to be initiated slowly and carefully. Once the CHANGE is made, everyone will take credit for the idea.
- People occasionally bring their dogs during the week when volunteering at the church.
- There are at least five senior citizens who are bilingual.
- There are at least five members who served in the armed forces during a war (both men and women).
- Pick up trucks have gun racks in the back

Well, there you have it - at least some of the characteristics that I have observed in small rural churches. Small churches and their quirkiness are not for everyone, but I, for one, love ours and especially the ability of our members to laugh at themselves. This is important in any church. In conclusion, a rural ministry may not be heaven, but, on a clear day, there are those who feel you can see it from there.

For where two or three are gathered together in My name, I am there in the mist of them.   (Matt. 18:20)

THE HUGGY, KISSY WOMAN

Garrison Keillor is a well known storyteller who has made fun of Lutherans for years. He is not a Lutheran. However, on a list comprised by one Lutheran observing other Lutherans, he listed the following characteristics (among others).
1. Lutherans believe in prayer but would practically die if asked to pray aloud.
2. Lutherans feel that applauding for their children's choirs would make them too proud and conceited.
3. Lutherans think that the Bible forbids them from crossing the aisle while 'passing the peace'.
4. Lutherans still serve Jell-O in the proper liturgical color for the season and think that peas in a tuna noodle casserole adds too much color.
5. Lastly, if the pastor says something really funny during the sermon, Lutherans feel free to smile as loudly as they can! (Sent from the internet, Sept. 13, 2004)

If you get the impression that Lutherans are reserved and a little on the conservative side, you are probably underestimating the situation. Having attended a Lutheran parochial school and college, having taught in Lutheran Schools, having married a Lutheran minister, and being rather shy on the inside, the Lutheran church is as familiar and comfortable to me as my mother's kitchen.

When I became one of the first women principals in a Lutheran School, the minister (who was old enough to be my father) sat me down for a little talk.

"Now that you are principal of the school," he said, "as pastor of this congregation there are times that we will need to meet together. Because we are of different genders, there are some precautions that must be observed. One: Whenever we meet in an office, the door must remain open so that the secretary and anyone passing by will be able to observe that everything is 'above board'. Two: If we need to attend a conference together, we must never be seen riding alone together in a car. Therefore, my wife will always accompany us. Three: And now that you are a leader of the church, you must be friendly and polite to everyone, but do not signal out anyone to be your special friend to avoid jealousy and evil talk. It is best to have a social life outside of the church membership. We can't be too careful."

You get the picture, and when Lutherans are uncomfortable even crossing the aisles to shake hands, you can imagine the effect that a 'huggy kissy woman' might have on the church body. This is Martha's (a sister in ministry) story.

Everything seemed to be going well in the new church for the first three years, then enter 'the huggy, kissy woman'. A 'huggy, kissy woman' is a warm, fuzzy, friendly person who is free with her hugs and kisses. Edith was a new member not only to the church but to Lutheranism. She became acquainted with the minister when he comforted her through her mother's illness and then burial. Edith and her husband, and later her children and their families, began attending and then joined the church.

Martha and Edith soon became good friends and enjoyed working together. Edith also enjoyed working with the pastor and spent a lot of time volunteering in the office and throughout the church, a service much appreciated because 'the need was great, but workers were few'. However, and here comes the big HOWEVER.

Edith was a 'huggy, kissy woman,' and her appreciation for and admiration of the minister was easy to see. This is common to those in human services, e.g., doctors, psychologists, counselors, teachers, ministers, etc.

In Martha's church, it is common practice for the ushers to dismiss the congregation row by row at the conclusion of the service. The minister shakes hands with each departing member, except for Edith who hugged and kissed him goodbye whenever she was at church. Granted, the kiss was just on the cheek; nevertheless, it's not how things are done in this church. After this had gone on for a while, Martha shared her story with me and asked for advice. I suggested that Martha talk to her husband about it and suggest that he 'discourage' the hugging and kissing.

Several months later, Martha shared that her husband felt it was all innocent and that he did not want to offend a new member. She noticed that Edith was now filling in for the church secretary and saw the familiarity with which she conversed with the minister on personal matters even during church dinners. The developing friendship now worried Martha to the point that she was losing sleep at night.

I explained that 'holy kissing' is practiced in some churches, but usually among members of the same sex. It is also just a cultural practice among different groups of people. Since Edith was new to the Lutheran Church and its practices, maybe it would help if what was considered acceptable behavior in this church be explained to her from a cultural point of view, by the minister. Another four months went by and Martha, exhausted from a lack of sleep, time in prayer, and a constant 'gnawing feeling' in the pit of her stomach, again shared with me. Her husband had again declined to talk to Edith, saying that his wife was just 'making a mountain out of a mole hill'.

Martha explained her concern that Edith's open and obvious affection could only lead to hurt, how she as his wife was already hurt that he would not gently put an end to the displays of affection. She offered an ultimatum that he should speak to Edith, or she as his wife would. When he continued to ignore the situation as 'harmless', Martha called Edith's home to make an appointment. She lay awake that night, composing exactly what she would say. She did not want to offend or lose a friend, but the behavior needed to be stopped for a number of reasons.

A week later, as Martha and I were having lunch together, she explained how she had spent hours rehearsing exactly what she would say, being very tactful. She would explain Lutheran customs at their church. While driving to the church, she tried to anticipate what Edith's reaction might be so as to know how to respond. While parking the car, she explained (with some embarrassment) that her last thought was, "What if she becomes angry? What if she pulls out a gun and shoots me?" Irrational? Well, at least the part about the gun; however, she had been struggling with this for over a year and wanted to be prepared for anything. Praying yet again for guidance, she met Edith in the church conference room.

Edith smiled nicely and said, "What did you want to meet about?"

And, in Martha's words, "she lost it". All the practicing, all the planning, all the lost sleep, all the praying - she just blurted out, " You have got to stop hugging and kissing my husband!"

Edith laughed and said, "O.K. Is that all? Done." No anger, no tears, no fight, NO GUN! End of story! Thank you, Jesus!

Martha is confident that no other inappropriate behavior occurred between them, but is glad she had 'the little talk' with Edith before it could possibly get out of control or cause 'damage' within the church.

Anyone in a position of authority and service must be very careful of how 'things' might be interpreted or viewed by those that look to them for leadership. If you are a minister's wife, you may have already encountered a 'huggy, kissy woman' and have advice to share from your own experience. Perhaps, depending on the cultural ethnicity of your church, this may be the norm. If you haven't encountered this situation, you may. If you are struggling with what to do with a similar situation, maybe this story and the following advice might be of help.

1. Unless the woman is the age of your mother or grandmother, if hugging and kissing is <u>not the custom or culture of your church</u>, nip it in the bud. Don't take the chance, and don't wait for a year. Be safe, not sorry.

2. Understand that the behavior may be very innocent and just a difference of cultural backgrounds, but could still hurt your husband's reputation.

3. Explain your feelings to your husband and ask him to discourage and stop the inappropriate display of affections, as of now! He should be the one to do this and immediately upon his wife's request.

4. I again emphasize that your husband should be the one to gently explain his position as minister and appropriate behavior as such . If for some reason, he is unable/unwilling to do this, then with prayer and guidance, you must explain the situation in private to the person as soon as possible.

5. Continually pray for help, understanding, and guidance.

6. If you need to talk to someone about it, make it someone <u>outside of your church</u> that will keep your confidence.

7. Keep it private and confidential. Keep the reputation of your husband and friend safe.

8. If you are the one to confront 'huggy kissy woman' be up front about how you feel and the reasons that you think a 'hands and lips off policy' is best to be maintained.

9. Thoughts might enter your mind such as "am I just giving into the sin of jealousy" or "am I just making a mountain out of a mole hill". Maybe, however, 'smoke sometimes has a way of developing into fire'. In ministry, it is best to ere on the side of caution when so many eyes are watching you.   If it is inappropriate, then it is inappropriate. End of story.

"Do not lay hands on anyone hastily, nor share in other people's sins; keep yourself pure."
I Timothy 5:22

ANOTHER PATH

At one time the Lutheran Church had more schools than any other Protestant Religion in America, and was superceded only by the Catholic Church. Lutheran schools accompanied Lutheran Churches from their early beginnings in America. At that time, the minister was also the teacher. The purpose of these schools was and is to train up the children in the faith of their parents, to preserve the faith. In more recent years, the purpose of the schools has extended to include ministry to those outside of the church as well as a form of evangelism.

I am a product of such a school. Coming from a Methodist family, my four older brothers all attended public schools; but for me, God had chosen another path. I attended a two room Lutheran School from grades one to six, and it has made all the difference. Kindergarten and grades one and two were taught in one room by Mrs. Forbes and grades three, four, five, and six were taught in the 'upper room' by Mr. Forbes. My grade had the largest number of students in the history of the school, twelve!

At St. John School, I learned to work quietly and concentrate while other grades were being taught. I learned to be an independent learner while also helping others to learn. I learned to be responsible for those younger than myself. And by the time I graduated from

St. John's, I was well versed in <u>Luther's Small Catechism</u> and knew the morning liturgy and many hymns from memory just from rote learning. Gym consisted of playing softball and games in a nearby empty field that was donated for that use. Occasionally we played other games, but mostly it was softball.

Special things that I remember included doing bulletin boards; and at times, I was sent into the 'little room' to help the little kids with reading. Each day at lunch time, Mr. Forbes (the upper grades teacher and principal) would choose a different 'little kid' to come up, blow out the match he used to light his pipe, and sit and talk to him on his lap while he had his after lunch 'smoke'. It was a special honor for each of us, especially for those of us who didn't have a caring father at home. It was a different time and a different school!

After sixth grade, I attended the local public junior and high schools. The Idyllic life at St. Johns was over, and culture shock set in with a vengeance with well over a 1,000 students in each school. Nevertheless, the lessons and experiences that I had at St. Johns has remained with me throughout life and has seen me through more than one difficult time. People sometimes question me about the validity of the curriculum that was taught at St. Johns. It consisted mostly of "readin', 'riting, 'rithmetic, and religion". I only know it never kept me from being an honor student throughout junior and high school, becoming a Lutheran teacher, getting a Masters degree in administration, becoming a principal in a Lutheran school, getting a PhD in curriculum and instruction, teaching in a Christian College, writing Christian curriculum, serving as a missionary, writing for publication, and doing countless other things that I thought I would ever do. More importantly, it helped to establish a personal relationship with Jesus Christ that has continued throughout my life.

I graduated from St. John's Lutheran School but never left the church. I chose to be confirmed at the church and my mother chose to do the same. One brother later married a girl from our church and also became a member. They have three children also brought up in the Lutheran Church. I went to a Lutheran college- Bronxville then River Forest where I met my husband. We taught in Lutheran Schools and put our two children through twelve years of Lutheran education,.

EPILOGUE: I later learned that my **St. John Lutheran School** was only open for a few years. It closed three years after I graduated from sixth grade, but it was there for me and others who attended the school. I can't think back on those early days without a smile on my lips and a tear in my eye.

Mr. Forbes went blind due to sugar diabetes and had to quit teaching after I completed the fourth grade. I cried when he left. On my walks home from high school, I used to visit the Forbes at least once a month and maintained contact with them until both joined our Lord in heaven.

My family: my husband went on to become a minister, and I have yet another role to play, that of a minister's wife. We currently have two grandsons attending a Catholic School and one attending a Lutheran Schools.

Christianity today: God chose a different path for me than what might have otherwise been chosen. I learned a lot in that little school: the most important of which is that Jesus is my Savior. It has not always been an easy path to walk, but it is one that leads to eternal salvation.

I recently learned that in the United States, approximately 75% of the Builder Generation (1925-1944), attended a Christian Church on a regular basis. Of the Boomer Generation (1945-1967), 50% belonged to a Christian Church. That percentage dropped to approximately 25% with the X Generation (1968 - 1999), and to **6% with the new Millennials** (2000 -). I repeat 6%! If ever there was a need for Christian Schools, it is now!

In the only nation described as 'The Christian Nation', the fastest growing religion in America today is Islam. Our forefathers and mothers knew that the future of the church is in the hands of the youth, and they supported Christian education. One hour of 'God' a week is not enough to combat the evils of this world. I know only too well that the financial cost of a Christian education requires some sacrifice, but not nearly the cost of not knowing Christ and his sacrifice for us. .

"Therefore you shall lay up these words of mine in your heart and in your soul, and bind them as a sign on your hand, and they shall be as frontlets between your eyes. You shall teach them to your children, speaking of them when you sit in your house, when you walk by the way, when you lie down, and when you rise up/.And you shall write them on the doorpost of your house and on your gates." (Deut. 11:18 -20)

ONE MAN AT THE END OF THE HALL

"We are fools for Christ's sake . . . " (I Cor 4:10)

It was the last day at Luther Memorial Camp in Southern Ohio. Students and teachers from different schools, as well as general campers of all ages, were gathered for a farewell devotion when in walked the clowns. Clowns! At a worship service! Who ever heard of such a thing! Sacrilege!

Actually, the liturgical clown used to be called the 'Holy Interrupter' and appeared frequently, briefly, and unexpectedly in early churches to emphasize a religious point. It forces the worshiper to think about what is happening and what worship should mean to God's people. The clown, in helping to remind us of our humanity, also shows us how we can praise God through actions and happenings without the use of speaking. (Hummm. More action, less talk. Maybe there is something to that).

Since the Liturgical Clown (or Clown for Christ as it is sometimes called) is a mime, there was no sound or wiggling during this service. Imagine 300 students and teachers sitting still and silent with their eyes glued to a troupe of clowns in an outdoor setting for an hour. Impossible? POSSIBLE! However, the students ranged in ages from six to fourteen. What could they possibly learn about

God from this 'entertaining' performance? We were about to find out.

After the clowns departed, other camp counselors came forward to 'debrief' the message. "What did you just see?"

"What was happening?"

"What were the clowns trying to tell us?"

"What did you just learn?"

"What does God want us to know/do" I sat spell bound. These same junior high students who are sometimes reluctant to become involved in discussion, now had lots to say. But what could a six year old learn from clowns? Plenty. It was fascinating how they saw and interpreted vital messages that older minds completely overlooked. It was powerful! I just had to share what I had just experienced with our entire school and church when we got back to Cleveland. But how? Bring on the grease paint!

One day, quite by accident, I discovered that someone was teaching others to use clowning as part of their worship service. The instructor had actually gone to Clown College; knew how to juggle, to make balloon animals, to do magic, and was a musician and liturgist for his Catholic church. WOW! Sign me up!

All those extra things are nice and can come in handy when you are visiting the children's ward in a hospital, but they are not necessary. I cannot juggle. I tried and tried, but invariably, the bean bags ended up falling down the top of my bib overalls. The kids thought it was funny. On the subject of balloon animals: those long skinny balloons are REALLY HARD to blow up. It took me several minutes to blow one up. Twisting the balloons into a shape was no problem except the squeaking of the balloons made me squint and when I would invariably break one, I nearly jumped out my trousers every time! I was a failure as a circus clown, but the kids thought I was hilarious.

I was taught to 'look for the child' within myself, and let her come out and that the clown would define herself and her name. It generally takes at least three months. Sound like something from the Twilight Zone? At the end of three months, my clown had emerged. Not what I would have expected, but definitely my own style. I gave her the name of 'Addy' short for Adonai (the love of Christ). Addy was a bag woman who wore old clothes that I had at home: an old pair of baggy big overalls from my husband, a pair of my son's big old sneakers, a 'Joseph's' coat from my first try at knitting (colorful but kinda warped), a favorite floppy beach hat, and a stripped 'T' shirt. Addy was gentle, shy, comfortable in her own space, and non threatening. She was the 'inner' me, and it was very 'freeing' to let Addy come out and just be herself. Addy ended up doing school, church, and Christian conference presentations. An interesting discovery I made was, that even though I did many 'clown services' within my own church and day school, it was over a year before anyone discovered that Addy was the minister's wife!

One day outside one large conference center where many different meetings were taking place, Addy was sitting on the steps eating cold baked beans out of can (yes, Addy and I both like cold beans out of a can). I was surprised at how many people stopped to talk to Addy on their way in. They actually came out of their way over to where she was sitting to talk. It didn't bother them that she was a mime. She listened to what they had to say, and they left with a smile. There's a lesson in that. Maybe we should all talk less and listen more!

A 'Walk About' is something a clown does while just walking around prior to a service or when just 'being' (like sitting on some steps, minding your own business, eating your beans.) One effective 'walk about' involves an index card with two words written on it: 'For two cents I would give you a hug.' Now, here is the clincher: two pennies are glued to the card. The clown hands the card to a passerby. The passerby takes the card, reads it, ponders it for a moment, and then generally a broad smile of comprehension spreads across his face; and he or she hands the card back to the clown expecting what happens next: the clown gives that person a big hug. (Hugs from Christian clowns are acceptable.) Occasionally, a person would hand back the card and just walk away, but that was very seldom. I was surprised at how many people would just 'soak up' and lose themselves in that clown hug, occasionally taking the card back just to get a second hug. Lesson learned: Talk less, hug more! There are so many people out there that just need a hug to keep them going.

One day, my teenage son announced that he too would like to become a 'Clown for Christ'. My former instructor was now holding a class for clowns and their protégés. We signed up. After some time and my son's own clown had emerged, the master clown turned us all lose in a hospital. Addy watched as the others joyfully set off down the halls in the children's wing with their bag of tricks (balloons, bean bags, etc.). Addy watched them go, and then silently went down a hall where none had chosen to go. With son in tow, she shyly peeked in the rooms they passed, and then lead him into a quiet room with just one patient, a very elderly man. They apparently were no longer in the children's wing.

The very old man, who appeared to be sleeping, slowly opened his eyes, looked at the two unexpected visitors and smiled. "You remind of my granddaughter," he said in a voice barely audible. Not knowing what else to do, Addy held a glass of water that was on his tray while he slowly sipped through the straw. My son, in the meantime, was deftly forming a dog out of a slender balloon and placed it on the tray. The old man smiled and then said something we weren't expecting, "I am dying. Father, would you please pray for me." To this day, I don't know why he thought Addy was a priest, but being a mime, she did the only thing she could think to do. Addy took his hand in hers and while she and her son bowed their heads, she said a silent prayer. To indicate the prayer was over, she made the sign of a cross on his forehead.

"Thank you," he said. "Your visit has meant the world to me. Now I can die in peace."

Addy and son, seeing the other clowns smiling and bounding down the hallways, walked silently back to the appointed debriefing room. Happy clowns smiled as each told their experiences. Last was Addy and son. Addy slowly told their experience of one man at the end of the hall, leaving all in silence. Do I believe God directed us to that room? Yes, I do. Did mother and son share something very special together that day about ministry. Without a doubt. Thank you, Jesus. May God be praised!

TODAY IS MONDAY

"It is God who arms me with strength;, and makes my way perfect." Psalm18:32

Today is Monday, the day after another very interesting and busy weekend. On Friday evening there was a wedding rehearsal and the rehearsal dinner; Saturday morning, a funeral and a reception following it. The wedding in the afternoon was in a neighboring town along with its reception. On Sunday, the Lord's Day, we had four services in the morning with a doughnut hour between services. After church, we only had one obligation before we could relax for the rest of the day and call our kids.

As we settled into reading the Sunday paper, the phone rang, and I heard my husband say, "I'll be right over."

"Now what?" I heard myself asking.

My husband stated, "Oh, it was Grace notifying me that George just passed away while taking his afternoon nap."

I thought to myself, 'Poor George. He must have just given up after his wife died last week.' After a quick change of clothing, off my husband went in his little Ford Focus to comfort the family for an hour, or perhaps the whole evening.

Today is Monday. Ah, what a beautiful day it is. I should be able to get all my planned activities done today. However, as I look at the clock on the wall I realize that it's nearly noon and soon my husband will be home for lunch. I wonder how his morning has gone; I know he planned to study for his three midweek Bible studies that he teaches during the course of the week and also spend time to prepare for the voters meeting tonight. Oh, I think I hear him coming in the door, and he's earlier than usual. It's good that I put a salad together for him before I got busy with my writing duties. Now as we eat, I hope that we can finally talk; and oh yes, I must ask him if he wants me to go shopping with him to buy the hotdogs and their fixings for the Wednesday night Bible study celebration he promised the group last week.

I greet him with my usual, "Hi Honey! How did your morning go? You're early."

"Well", he answers in a rather somber voice. "Do you remember the news this morning about that man who got hit and killed during the night while walking along route 90?"

"Yes," I reply,

"Well, he is a member of our church."

"Who is it?" I ask rather alarmed "Is he someone I know?"

My husband answers, "No, it was Ralph Ericson's eighteen year old son."

I quickly blurt out, "Oh no, what a tragedy for the family! How are his folks doing? "

My husband senses the anxiety and perhaps over identification in my voice as he replies, "Not so well. You know Karen, his mother has not been well, and I'm worried about her."

Well, our week is beginning to shape up with two funerals, three Bible studies, and at least two meetings, and yet another wedding coming up.

After the news at lunch, my heart is heavy even though the day began in a quiet and peaceful way. I should be able to concentrate on my planned activities for the afternoon, but the death of that teenager looms in my mind. I realize that I often over relate with our members in their time of grief. I have been a pastor's wife for over thirty- five years, and still can not get through a funeral without tears. However, today I am thankful that it's summer so that I can attend these events, because when fall arrives I will again be teaching full time.

This is just an example of the life a pastor and his family lives when serving a large congregation made up of nearly three thousand souls. You love them, and you constantly try to get to know them. Some folks move and others come in to take their place, so your church picture book is never, never up to date. Along with keeping up with my husband's busy schedule throughout the years, we also had the children and their special events that we always tried to attend. And, yes I have been a working pastor's wife. I taught in an elementary grade school for years before going back to school to get my Master's degree and finally finish my Ph.D.; all the while working full time and being my husband's help mate.

No, life has not been boring, nor do we take any day for granted. There is not a day I do not, upon rising, thank the Lord for a new day, and that we will have the strength, wisdom, and health to serve Him well. Life has been a blessing to us, and God has blessed us richly by giving us His special people to serve and minister to for over the thirty plus years. One might ask; Has it been difficult, and have there been hardships over that time span? Yes, there have been many times when God's people have been less than kind, loving, considerate, and understanding of us. There have been many occasions when I prayed fervently that Satan would have no power over us and God's church, because the circumstances were so very difficult to deal with. Ten years ago the Lord gifted my husband with ten more years of life after having emergency quadruple by pass surgery. And yes, our children did both experience many of the same challenges of growing up that other people's children do along with the challenges of being PKs(Preacher Kids). However, God is faithful in his promise when he instructs us to 'Train a child in the way that he should go, and when he is old he will not turn from it' Proverbs 22: 6

My husband and I are so blessed. Each of our children has grown up to be very dedicated in their love and service to the Lord. Our son faithfully serves his Lord through witnessing to his own sons and working within his church as a lay person. Our daughter and her wonderful husband travel nationally and internationally serving the Lord through their teaching and music ministries to both youth and adults.

Today is Monday, and it is *'the day the Lord has made; we will rejoice and be glad in it. Psalm 118:24.* We will continue to use our gifts and talents, regardless of how tired we become, because God has called us and given us the privilege to serve Him. I am confident that He will continue to guide and give us the strength to meet His challenges each day; and as Christians, it is our duty to always keep our eyes upon Jesus.

CALLED TO CARE, LOVE, LISTEN, and HELP

As a pastor's wife, I have had many opportunities to care, love, listen, and help others. Not every situation involved people from our church, but in many instances, those with whom I worked or simply met in a women's restroom at a restaurant. I have always realized that God has called me to fulfill His work for individuals who needed a listening ear and a helping hand in order to get through their challenging times. Thus, when I first heard about the Stephen Ministry and learned about its mission, I knew that God was calling me at this juncture of my life to use me in this special ministry.

The mission of Stephen Ministries is to help congregations equip God's people for spiritual growth and Christ-centered, practical ministry in today's world. (Kenneth C. Haugh, 1984)

What does it take to become a Stephen Minister? The Stephen Series is a complete system developed to train and organize lay persons to provide One -On - One Christian care in and around congregations, with an emphasis on confidentiality. This ministry is named after Stephen, the first lay person chosen by the Apostles to care for the needs of that early congregation (Acts 5:1-6).

The ministry was started by Dr. Kenneth C. Haugk (1984), a St. Louis Pastor and Clinical Psychologist. As a parish pastor in 1975, he realized that the needs for care in his congregation exceeded what he alone could provide, so he drew on his psychological and theological background to train nine members as 'Stephen Ministers' to assist him with pastoral care. Later that year, he and his wife Joan founded Stephen Ministries to bring this caring ministry to other congregations.

The Stephen Series has now been implemented in more than 9,000 congregations representing more than 100 Christian denominations. More than 450,000 lay persons have been trained as Stephen Ministers, who in turn have ministered to nearly a million care receivers.

Stephen Ministry is for people who want someone to care, to listen, to share God's love during or throughout confusing, stressful, or lonely times. Stephen Ministry helps meet the needs of individuals who are hospitalized, terminally ill, bereaved, in a crisis, new members of the church, disabled, homebound, lonely, in a spiritual crisis, looking for a caring, Christian friend.

- Is life more than you can handle alone right now?
- Are your health, your attitudes, or your relationships suffering?
- Are you adjusting to a new job, change in marital status, a serious illness, the death of a loved one, a recent move?
- Would you like to have someone in your life who really cares? (Haugk, 1984) Everyone goes through difficult times. Having someone to care, to listen, to share God's love with you can help you get through the confusion, stress, or loneliness you may be experiencing. Our Stephen Ministers are caring church members who offer one-on-one caring relationships for those in need.

A Stephen Minister is:
- A child of God who walks beside a hurting person.
- A caring Christian friend who really listens
- A lay person who has received 50 hours of training in how to provide distinctively Christian care

A Stephen Minister is not:
- A counselor or therapist
- A problem-solver
- A casual visitor (1984)

The Stephen Ministry is designed to provide one-on-one Christian care to individuals facing life challenges or difficulties. Stephen Ministers, supervised lay people, receive 50 hours of instructor-led training and make a commitment for two years to train and serve. Among the training topics are:
- Feelings: Yours, Mine, and Ours
- The Art of Listening
- Distinctively Christian Caring
- Maintaining Boundaries in Caregiving
- Confidentiality
- Ministering to Those Experiencing Grief
- Caring for People Before, During,, and After Hospitalization

As I have stated, I am totally convinced that this is the Ministry the Lord has called me for at this juncture in my life. I have often had the privilege of witnessing God's mighty working in the lives of those who are for some reason challenged or hurting. My constant prayer is:

"Send me and use me, O Lord; My time is in Your hands."
Dr. Faith Wesolik

8

COMMUNITY

"Friendships multiply joys, and divide griefs."
- Henry George Bohn

THE HOUSE THAT GOD BUILT

After three years of trying to adopt, we finally received word from David Livingston Missionary Foundation that a little girl had been selected for us. She was six months old and it would take nine months to go through the paper work necessary for an international adoption. Nine months. The same length of time for a child to be born to us. Nine months to prepare for her coming. Nine months to find a home with an additional bedroom. Then a friend told us about an old abandoned farm house that was on five acres of land and was for sale.

It was a "handyman's delight" for sure, but it was something we could afford and something we could fix. Our first surprise was that the basement actually had a concrete floor beneath all the dirt; and with much cleaning, the old coal bin became an ideal storage area for canned goods. Then my husband paneled the walls, put in a drop ceiling, a new furnace, and laid linoleum. This basement became Anthony's Acres Christian Preschool.   My husband and I were both Lutheran school teachers at the time, but since I was temporarily a stay-at- home mom for our three year old son and soon to be daughter, we devised a way that I could stay at home with our children and still teach others.

The thirsty bare walls devoured gallons of paint as my husband worked outside in the sun. I became an expert at taping and "mudding" new wall board. We stripped and stained and varnished hard wood and new doors. I cleaned and painted and papered the walls. At night, I worked on sewing curtains made from new sheets. Our new daughter arrived in early December just in time to move into the newly prepared home. A neighbor walked a mile in the snow just to welcome us with homemade blood sausage, and contentment filled my soul as we settled our family, including Fritz the dog and Shoo Shoo our Siamese cat, into our "Currier and Ives' farmhouse.

In the spring, new broods hung close to clucking hens, tulip poplars lined the drive way, and white petals littered the lawn. Later, honeysuckles bloomed on the fence, and pink mimosas attracted hummingbirds to the front yard. Fruits and vegetables ripened in the garden, and sun streamed in my attic sewing room. We gorged ourselves on homemade applesauce, Keifer pears, and the largest, sweetest blackberries in all of Missouri. George, our now four year old, climbed the trees; and took care of chickens while Ember (our daughter) made castles in the sand box. I never knew life could be so good.

Then winter came once again. It snowed for thirty days and nights non stop, but we were snug by our fireplace in our cozy home; however, it wasn't so cozy for the wild life. A hungry bobcat got into our hen house and slaughtered twelve of the poulets that we had raised from chicks, and hungry mice ate unfortunate kin caught in traps before we could empty the traps each morning.

Late one afternoon, as the children played by the fireplace and I was sewing nearby on the kitchen table, I noticed smoke. Thinking that I had a green log in the fireplace, I stirred the ashes, and opened the door to let out the smoke. I closed it again shortly after. I was busy back at sewing when a knock came on the door.

"Lady, your house is on fire!" a man informed me.

I hurried the children to the neighbors and asked that she call the fire department and my husband who was still at work. I called for Shoo Shoo. Thinking she might be asleep in my bedroom, I started down the hall when I realized that the floors were too hot for my feet. Assuming the fire had started in the schoolroom below, I rushed outside to the outdoor entrance taking a wet towel with me. Opening the door, thick billows of smoke rushed out burning my eyes making it difficult to see. I quickly grabbed the hose, turned on the water, wrapped the wet towel around my mouth so that I could breathe, and entered the burning room trying to reach the spot where I saw flames. With burning eyes and lungs, I wasn't able to get far. I threw the hose as close to the fire as I could, then followed it back outside in time to hear the windows exploding in the house.

A neighbor helped to remove a new rocking chair from the living room and placed it by a tree in the front yard. Only fifteen minutes had elapsed since I was made aware of the fire. The house, breeze way, and garage were now fully engulfed by flames; and the wind was carrying sparks.   The fire trucks arrived and began hosing down the buildings of our closest neighbor to keep those from catching fire also. The rocking chair, our only new piece of furniture, by the tree, burst into flames from the heat. Onlookers by the road were told to move their cars for fear their gas tanks might explode. My husband arrived from school forty-five minutes later to see a deep gorge filled with burning timbers where our house had once been. It had all happened so quickly. The cause of the fire was later attributed most likely to hungry mice chewing wires above the drop ceiling in the school room.

The next day, the newspaper read "Fire destroys home in country. Smouldering ruins are all that remain. Another structure lost to fires in rural Cape County." Had the fire occurred 13 days later, our insurance would have tripled to cover the expenses of the new furnace and remodeling, but the fire occurred before the new policy took effect. We were given $25,000.00 to cover the home and everything in it.   But the story doesn't end there.

That night, at a neighbor's home, I lay awake wondering what to do. In a few hours the sun would be up; and we would have no place to live, no clothes to wear, no belongings, very little money, and I would have no ID. We would have to start all over from scratch. Just how do you go about doing that? I prayed to God for guidance, and the answer came. We still had our family. We still had our land. We even still had our chicken coop with chickens; and in the morning, we would find that we still had our dog! I did not want to leave our "home".

The insurance paid for us (and Fritz the dog) to stay in a motel for several weeks. Because we lived outside of city limits we were allowed to put a trailer on our property. A kindhearted salesperson sold us a small new furnished mobile home for cost ($4,000.00). We stayed in the hotel until we were able to get gas, electricity, and water hookups installed to support the mobile home. My husband had to keep teaching, so I dealt with newspapermen who wanted the story and who advertised our need. A friend had offered her home for the collection of donations, and within four days, her basement looked like a Good Will Store. When I arrived, everything a person could need was there and arranged in categories, by size, etc. Marge had worked overtime in its organization. There were so many donations from people we didn't even know (in most cases) that after we were settled again, Marge opened her "basement supply center" to four other families that had home fires shortly after ours and their needs were also met.

When we received the insurance money, my husband opened a new bank account and we received a silver plated tray with eight goblets as a gift. Later when construction men were working at the site, it made us laugh that we had nothing in which to offer them a drink other than those silver goblets! A month later, the remains of all our possessions had evaporated, melted, or were reduced to ashes in the basement of our former home. There was about a foot of water covering everything, and the remains were still smoldering. Nothing was salvageable, but God had been gracious. I grieved for only one loss that could not be replaced: Shoo Shoo. Three years before, I had had a miscarriage. Shortly following the loss of that child, I obtained Shoo Shoo, a sickly little kitten that nearly died. Shoo Shoo became the baby I had lost, and we were bonded as close as any mother and child. Shoo Shoo was the only thing that I lost in the fire that couldn't be replaced, and I mourned her as I would a child.

Within weeks, we were back at "home" in our fully furnished mobile home. People had donated clothes, dishes, linens, silverware, toys, fabric, whatever. We had everything we needed and more, including a little humor. I had bought a dozen new chicks and when the weather dipped down again, I housed them in our trailer bathroom until the weather warmed. They grew more quickly than I expected and occasionally got out of their container and perched on my husband's head when he was "indisposed" - a feat that he didn't find amusing or appreciate, I might add.

Our church let me use a room to continue teaching preschool. My preschool students came from various church backgrounds. One of my student's was a Mormon, and a group of Mormons threw a surprise party for us where we received more new gifts than we received at our wedding reception. One person even brought a new fire engine for our kids to play with, and I was able to quip, "Where was this when I needed it!" Other parents from a variety of churches chipped in with financial donations.

In the spring, the damaged concrete from the basement and the remaining ashes had to be removed before we could begin rebuilding. Another friend found a person who was offering $500.00 for land fill, so we didn't have to pay to have it removed. Once the basement had been excavated, my husband, teachers, church members, and children came with wheelbarrows to line the hole with gravel that was necessary before concrete could be laid. It was hard work! It was a happy day when the foundation was finally poured.

Next, a contractor from our church offered to put up the frame of the house with no charge for labor. My husband and I did most of the finishing. (The farm house had taught us a lot!) When it came time to brick the front, a mason taught my husband how to lay brick which he later did. When it came time to shingle the roof, volunteers who had never roofed before lined up while my husband gave instructions prior to their climbing on the roof. Years later my husband liked to say that we had the only roof that waved at people as they went by! It was a friendly roof laid by friends, and it never leaked! Before winter again returned, the house was far enough along that we could move in. We sold the mobile home for a small profit to help pay some bills.

Hearing the story, people often ask how I felt about losing everything. " It must have been devastating". And they are surprised when I say, " It was a blessing."

"A blessing! How can you say it was a blessing?!" And I explain.

Our house was in a way a museum of things we had collected since we were kids, but didn't necessarily need. The little mobile home taught us a lesson. We don't "need" most of the "stuff" we have; we just "want it" and "collect it", then need a place to "store it", and "dust it". I was surprised to learn that our trailer provided and housed everything we needed. Things can sometimes be a burden or a habit or an obsession without our realizing it. Until you are faced with having nothing, do you really appreciate what you have and what is most important.

Being dependent on others teaches us humility and appreciation for those around us and sympathy for those who have less. We personally saw how good and caring people can be for total strangers in need. We experienced God's love, goodness, and kindness through the many people (as shown above) that He sent to help us. We " walked through the fire" and saw God. And when it comes down to it, only one thing is needful, and that is Jesus Christ.

"For He shall give His angels charge over you, To keep you in all your ways." (Ps. 91:11)

BLESSINGS FROM ABOVE

"For I was hungry and you gave Me food; I was thirsty and you gave Me drink; I was a stranger and you took Me in;"Matthew 25:35

It was 11:00 P.M., or nearly bedtime for our household, when the doorbell rang. As I meandered to the front door, I wondered who would be visiting at this hour. As I approached the front I could see through the windowed French doors that there was more than one person standing on our porch, in fact there were eight individuals. When I opened the door, a nice looking young man stepped forward, and stated, We are a Lutheran Youth Encounter Team, and we wonder if we could stay with you tonight?

Now, I was very familiar with these teams because our daughter had been on at least three of them. They were musical ministry teams who traveled specific areas of the United States and abroad which were assigned to them at their commissioning service. These kids were wonderful wholesome young Christians who gave a year or more of their lives in order to do this ministry. And, no, they did not receive huge wages for their services. Their return was in their proclamation of the Gospel message through word and song. I knew immediately that our daughter Katie had told them that if they were ever in our area our home would be open to them. So here they were, all eight of them needing a bed to sleep in and a few (many) bites to eat. Fortunately, I had gone to the grocery store that day so my pantry was well stocked and I had enough rooms for them to nest.

I got up early the next morning to prepare a simple breakfast for the team and some sandwiches for the road. They ate their breakfast and watched some TV before it was time for them to leave. As they packed up their van and left for their next gig, I could not help but to think that they were all great kids, and so much fun to have in our home. We had been so blessed to have a home that could accommodate groups, and our Katie certainly had the gift of hospitality, as we often housed teams that had no place to go for the night.

I cleaned up the kitchen and threw several loads of sheets in the washer and dryer before getting on with my day. That evening my husband and I ate dinner and then sat down to watch some of our favorite TV shows. While watching a commercial, my husband's attention was diverted to the breakfast room of our house. Suddenly he gasped, saying "Go get a bucket. The kitchen ceiling is falling down! " I turned to see what he was referring to, and saw a huge bulge in the ceiling area over our kitchen table. It was obvious that the only thing holding the ceiling up was our flowered wall paper that so beautifully decorated the ceiling in that room.

Directly above that room was a guest bathroom in the upstairs hallway. Upon further inspection of the problem, my husband called a man in our church who was a private building contractor, handy man, and an expert problem solver. He came over as quickly as he could, and together they decided that one of the bathroom fixtures was malfunctioning; we were collecting a huge amount of water which was only being held up with our wallpaper. The only solution would be to first release the water by cutting into my beautiful wallpaper and collecting the water in the buckets that I had managed to gather.

On a personal level, I was just sick about the situation, because

I had personally loved having that ceiling wall papered. Well, there was absolutely no time for me to argue other than to say, "Oh please don't cut the wallpaper." To say the least, my request went unheeded, and the paper was slashed. To my astonishment, water came gushing out like a geyser, and with it some of the wallboard also fell. Well, as the days went by, the bathroom problem was diagnosed as a weak pipe that had probably been over-loaded with TP, etc., and of course it sprung a huge leak.

As the story goes, we all lived happily ever-after. The ceiling was fixed, and I got to choose new wallpaper for my ceiling that was even more beautiful than its predecessor. I told my husband that the whole incident reminded me of one of my favorite childhood stories, that of Henny Penny when she yelled, " The sky is falling down; the sky is falling down!" As for us, the story ended well, and God's blessings continue to flow from above.

9

PARENTING IN THE PARSONAGE

"A child's mind is like a bank - whatever you put in, you get back in ten years, with interest."

-Frederic Wertham

AT THE FRONT OF THE CHURCH

BABIES: I grew up with kids in the church. The sound of a baby's wail made us all smile: that was the sound of the future generation that would carry on the work of the church. You hear no such sound in my present church of silvered haired seniors. Unfortunately, one or two of them actually complained about children in the church and discouraged the parents from bringing them. We never saw those parents and children in church again. Without children, churches die. Jesus said, "Suffer the little children to come unto me." And if that means "suffering" through a little noise and restlessness, so be it!

Today the discussion revolves around "At what age is it appropriate to bring a child to church?" I will never forget one family in particular at our first congregation. We were serving a rural church, and the Thimsens had seven children. In chronological order, the children's names were: Leanne, Lori, Lanette, Lynelle, Lorette, Lorna, and finally a boy: Luther. (They had a thing for the letter "L".) Rather than sit in the designated "children pews" at the back of the church, papa Thimsen and mama led those kids to the front, filling up the entire pew right in front of the pulpit. Not often, but on occasion, papa would been seen walking a sad looking child down the center aisle (it was always the center aisle) to the back of the church. In less than three minutes, they would walk back up the aisle into their pew, and all would be peaceful again.

One day I asked him if it would be easier to sit in the back of the church with the kids. "Nope," he said.

"Why not?" I asked.

"Well," he said. "At front they get to see everything that goes on: the babies being baptized, the acolytes doing their job, the choir singing, the pianist playing, the people taking communion, the Lambs' Talk, the minister preaching (and occasionally looking down at them), and occasionally a church mouse or a stray bird or fly that made it in the building. It keeps their attention and they learn all that goes on in a church."

It made sense to me, and I decided to follow the Thimsen example. Both our children were brought up in the front of the church with keys to play with and Cherrios to munch. It took only a few trips to the back of the church for them to learn proper behavior. Among other things, they learned to go to the bathroom right before and after church, not during. They learned the liturgy and parts of Christian songs before they could read. They enjoyed getting a close up look of babies being baptized, and they learned about the different "services" that they would perform in the church one day. Most of all, they learned that they were part of a very large church family that loved them and saw all that they did in the front pew!

One day when I was sharing a story designed for older kids and adults with the congregation, I was surprised that I also held the attention of the little ones. They seemed spellbound and afterwards could tell the story and what it meant to them. Kids are listening even when they don't appear to be, and they hear and understand more than we think. If you don't believe me, just try whispering to someone in the house someday! People like to say, "It takes a village to raise a child." I submit, "It takes a church to raise a child!" What is the proper age for children to begin attending church? My answer to that would be, "When they start breathing!"

TEENS: Needless to say, things have changed since I was a teen. In our church, disrespect among teens generally occurs most often with kids who have not been brought up in the church from infancy. The same teens who can sit for two hours in front of a movie or video game without getting up, are permitted to leave the church proper during the sermon under the guise of having to go to the bathroom and instead wander the halls, sometimes getting into mischief. Seldom do I see them sing or even participate in the service. They are there in body only visibly against their will by parents who are hoping the Holy Spirit will touch their lives.

I am astonished today at teens who have to be bribed by their parents to acolyte and then slouch at the front of the church trying to sleep, doodle, or play with a Game Boy in total disrespect for the Word. Additionally, such behavior sets a bad example for the younger children. Saddened and yes, angered, by such slovenly behavior, I was led to write a letter to the Board of Elders suggesting that a Guideline for Acolytes (and their parents) be written and included in instruction at the first year of confirmation. It has helped to solve the behavior, but I am not sure about the heart issue. It saddens me. It is more difficult for children to accept Christ as their personal Savior when parents have waited until their children are ready for confirmation to finally introduce them to God and His church.

Next year, the last three of our youth will be confirmed, and if they follow suit with the majority of their predecessors, that will be the last we see of them until they possibly want to get married. Some parents today feel once youth are confirmed, they are adults and are free to make their own decision about coming to church. Let's think about that. They are required to go to school. They cannot get a driver's license, or vote, or serve in the military, or get married, or smoke, or drink alcoholic beverages. To add to that list, their brains are only half developed. They are literally working with half a brain, but when it comes to church, some parents leave the decision to come to church up to their children. Our rule is, "As long as you live under my roof, you follow the rules and you go to church."

Prayer is no longer permitted in schools, support has been

dropped for Boy Scouts of America because they refuse to drop "for God" from their oath, Christmas displays are no longer permitted in our city squares, some religious groups swear to kill all Christians, school sporting events are held on Sundays during church time, and the list goes on; resulting in a dangerous, drastic decline of Christianity in America . I have taught school for forty-two years, and I have seen the changes over the years; and in my opinion, it hasn't been for the best. "It's a war out there." The Bible tells us to *"Train up a child in the way he should go, and when he is old he will not depart from it."* (Prov. 22:6)   Satan and the world are constantly fighting against Christianity. As parents, the least we can do is to provide our children with all the protection and ammunition we can for as long as we can to protect them from "the devil, the world, and our flesh." Am I biased on this issue? You betcha! I have seen the results!

PRANKS IN THE PARSONAGE

Now there might be such a thing as an angel PK (Pastor's Kid), but quite honestly, I have never met one; and if my own PK's were angels, one would have to question from which destination, above or below! However, having grown up with four older brothers, I learned a few tricks that enabled me to survive my brothers, teaching middle grade students, and yes, my own PK's. The secret to my success is to **"show no fear"**: not of the dark, heights, being locked in closets, scarey things, or being tickled until I wet my pants. I learned to control my impulses. The day that I announced that I was no longer ticklish and with upmost control succeeded in not laughing and wiggling or wetting my pants, was the day my brothers started looking for a new way to torment their little sister.

However, there is one fear that I still have not been able to completely control: the fear of things with more than four legs. Being a gardener, I have managed to flick them off without much ado as long as I do it quickly without thinking, but being surprised by one suddenly appear or jump on me is another matter. I am talking about BUGS. Big bugs, little bugs, bugs with hairy legs, evil little bugs that have nothing better to do than to walk on me! I seem to attract them. The day I was taking a bath when one landed in my bath water, and I screamed for my husband to get it out and exorcize it, my fate was sealed. My kids knew I had arachnid phobia !

From that day on, I never knew when or where a big hairy black spider would appear or be flung at me. To make matters worse, I had taken special care to raise my children so that they would have no irrational fear of BUGS! When tactic number one (show no fear) didn't work, I had to resort in self-defense to rule two: "retaliate to make them stop" ! Still, in all fairness, I gave them three chances to repent before I was forced to announce:

"Strike three! You have earned a retaliation! But not today, not tomorrow, maybe next week or next month, but when and where you least expect it, in a way you'll never expect. It will happen! Bug flinging is going to stop!"

"Oh, I am so scared," said my son through his laughter. "See me shaking from fear," Six foot teenage boys can be so obnoxious!

Summer and fall and "spider time" had passed. Winter was upon us. I was attending a Board of Education meeting that had lasted longer than usual into the evening. Leaving to go home, I was surprised to find that about three feet of snow had fallen during the time that we were in session, and it was still coming down, fast and furious. It was midnight before I made it home. I stepped out of my car to a breath-taking scene that can best be described in the words of Clement Moore: "The moon on the breast of the new fallen snow, gave a luster of midday to objects below."

Instinctively knowing that there would be no school the next day, I decided to give into my "inner child". I quietly woke my husband and convinced him to come outside to "play". Surprisingly, he agreed. First we made a snowman, then we threw snowballs at our neighbor's windows just so they would know it was snowing. (They thanked us in the morning, sorta). Then it hit me, retaliation time had arrived!

My husband and I carefully carried that snowman into my son's bedroom just to share the glory of the night snow! We placed it next to my sleeping son waiting for the reaction. Well, nothing sleeps as soundly as a teenage boy. We waited and waited and waited with the sleeping, melting snowman in the darkness. There was no fun in this, so we turned on his bedroom lights. Still no response. My husband took a picture of the "two" sleeping together, and when he still didn't wake up, we went to bed. Sometime later in the night, we heard a stir in his room, a sleepy "What?", and a cry of "MOM! That's not funny!" I could hear him escorting his sleeping partner to the outside and probably changing sheets, as I rolled over to go to sleep with a smile on my lips. Nothing tastes sweeter than a well executed lesson so obviously earned. Don't mess with Mom!

" 'Honor your father and mother' - which is the first commandment with a promise - That it may go well with you and that you may ENJOY LONG LIFE ON THE EARTH!" (Eph. 6:2-3)

PRANKS IN THE PARSONAGE II

POP! (As my daughter opened her bedroom door). **POP!** (As she opened her dresser drawer!) **POP!** (As she sat at the kitchen table!) **POP!** (As my husband stepped on the accelerator of his car). Each of these **POPs** was followed by an increasingly more exasperated cry of "George"! This was my son's first year away at college, and he had just come home on break, just to annoy us! While away, he had "discovered " what I call "poppers" and in the last four days he had been annoying everyone and animal in his path with his new prank. Like the old time caps, poppers had a small amount of gun powder in them, and any little force would result in a loud pop startling his most recent victim. (**POP!** (As I sat on the toilet seat!)

"That's it!" I yelled, pulling up my pants and chasing him down the hall where mother, father, and sister succeeded in tackling him long enough to confiscate the annoying bounty. "Strike three!" I yelled.

"Can't build a snowman in my bed this time," he retorted, "no snow!"

"Wipe that smirk off your face now," I said. "This calls for major retaliation!"

"Yeah, yeah, yeah," he said, "Bring it on!" (A big mistake on his part!)

You would think that by now he would know better than to challenge his mother. This took some major inspiration.

Thanksgiving, Christmas, and Easter all came and went without a hitch. George began to forget about the Popper incident, basking in his glory, and letting down his guard. Then came Spring, inspiration, and the" Reckoning" . No "sin" would go unpunished - like I promised: when he least expected it.

It was approaching nightfall in Hocking State Park. George had decided that he wanted to sleep in the two man tent by himself while my husband, daughter, and I shared the larger nylon backpacking tent. We were doing some primitive camping. My husband and I lay awake watching the last embers of our campfire slowly die out. In the background, I could hear the soft snoring of our son and daughter and familiar animal sounds from the deep woods. I slowly moved out of our tent.

"What are you doing?" my husband asked.

"Shhhhhh," I said, cautioning him not to wake the kids. "Just watch." I slowly crept toward my son's tent and placed a ring of marshmallows around his tent and leading into the open flap. I started back, when another thought occurred, and I went back to loosen the ropes on his tent stakes just for good measure.

"You are so bad," my husband said. "No wonder he is the way he is!"

All that remained was to stay awake and wait. We could hear them in the distance. My husband called them "Tecumseh and his raiding band!" The raccoons were coming. As a young girl, I had raised an orphan raccoon and knew all about them. They are from the bear family, and in the middle of a dark night, they sound very scarey as they converse while looking for food. Every camper is familiar with raccoons and knows, that despite their scarey sounds, they are easily chased away. One thing more: they love marshmallows!

We lay awake listening as the sounds got closer and closer. Our tent was facing our son's, and we were now lying low on our stomachs at our open door so as to better observe the "wildlife".

Around midnight, a mother coon and her three fairly large "youngin's" entered our campsite. We could hear them munching on the "mallows". One by one the marshmallows were devoured and they reached the opening of the tent. Not disturbed by our sleeping son, they entered to get the last of the tasty treats. We could hear the mother give instructions to the babies. It sounded like, "Stay away from the man. They can be unpredictable!"

At that point, our son must have awakened because we heard a low growly sound, this time from our son.

"What? What are you doing in here? Get out! Now! Shooo."

At this point he attempted to stand up. (Not a good idea in a small two man tent.) The racoons scurried off, taking the last of the marshmallows with them, and due to the loosened ropes (a brilliant last minute decision on my part, I might add), the tent collapsed on my son.

"Shhh, he'll hear us," my husband cautioned as I struggled to stifle my laughter.

In the darkness, I could hear our son trying to put his tent back up.

"I hear you, Mom, I know you did this! It ain't funny!"

My husband and I finally rolled over with satisfied smiles and quickly went to sleep.

EPILOGUE: When telling this story to friends, they usually give me a quizzical look and often say, "What is wrong with you people?!" You're not like any ministerial family we know! However, I love telling this story. It is my best "Gotcha", my masterpiece of creative lessons when up against teenager pranksters, my "Venus de Milo"! I learned from the best: my four "redneck" older brothers who taught me to enjoy nature and all of God's creation, that a family that plays together, stays together; and to never let your kids get the best of you! I did them proud!

"A joyful heart is like good medicine." (Prov. 17:22)

MIXED BLESSINGS

And all these blessings shall come upon you and overtake you, because you obey the voice of the Lord your God;" Deuteronomy 28:2 "

I woke up early, and opened the back door of my folks home. I thought about   how good it was to find the time to go home and see our folks. The morning was fresh with a smell of spring in the air. This was a familiar aroma to both my husband and me, as we both had grown up in the area. As I meditated, I somehow dreaded the next few hours, because today was the day we had to travel home to northern Missouri with a toddler and a nine-month-old baby. As most of you know, traveling with small children is a real challenge. However, we did manage to pack the car, say our goodbyes, and travel that day. As we neared home, my son announced that he was really, really thirsty. So like many good parents do, we stopped and had dinner, and each of us ordered a tall cold orange drink. My husband urged us to hurry, for as usual he had a church council meeting that evening.

As we neared our home, both children were ready to move out of their seat belts. After the car was unpacked, my husband gave us all a good-bye kiss and was off to his meeting in the next town.

It was my job to unpack, play with the kids, give them each a bath, and finally put them to bed. However, as the evening played out, our routine quickly would change.

After the goodbyes were said, James ran in the parsonage's living room which was decorated with a soft light green carpet, and threw up his supper along with the bright orange drink that he had gulped down. At that point, James badly needed to be cleaned up and tended to, so I plopped his little sister, Katie in her crib where she'd be safe. I hurried to not only help my poor sick James, but also knew that the carpet needed to be cleaned up quickly in order to get all traces of the bright orange color out of that light green carpet. In the back of my mind I knew the trustees would not appreciate a ruined carpet!

As I was nearly finished with the awesome tasks, Katie started to cry. I hurried up to her room to see what her problem was only to find out what my sweet little daughter had been doing to keep herself busy as I tended to her brother. As I walked closer to her, I was shocked to find out that she had not only filled her diaper, but had managed to finger paint its contents all around her crib and the walls, too. Yes, I faced another dilemma for now Katie badly needed a bath, and of course there were those green walls and the crib that also needed to be cleaned! At the end my mommy chores, I finally got both kids to bed and asleep. I thought to myself that they had really exhausted themselves and me with their flurry of sick activities that evening.

Not long after the major catastrophes had been solved, my happy husband came home with a smile on his face only to ask me if I'd had a good evening. At that moment, I broke down and cried. As I related the evening's activities to him, I felt a bit guilty. Had I not always thought that children were little blessings from God, and that being a pastor's wife was a special call from God? With guilt, I recalled a Bible verse I had committed to memory; *Proverbs 31:28 Her children rise up and call her blessed, and her husband also praises her.* However, that night I really, really had some serious doubts about these mixed blessings!

MY DADDY CAN DO ANYTHING

And you, fathers, do not provoke your children to wrath, but bring them up in the training and admonition of the Lord." Ephesians 6:4

Little boys often choose their father as their role model as they grow and develop. Once a child goes off to school, parents no longer can monitor everything that they say and do. So it was with little Zachary, when he started kindergarten in our Church's School. His favorite time of the week was the day the students had show' n tell. Like the other children in his class, Zach liked to take his most treasured item of the moment and tell about it. This Thursday, however, Zach had gone to school and left his treasured show' n tell bag on the kitchen counter. When he got to school, he realized his coveted item was not with him. Throughout the morning, he wondered what to use for his show'n tell that day. As the day moved on, Zach had to do some ingenious planning, and finally decided that he would do the tell rather than the show part of show n tell. When it was finally his turn to get up in front of his friends, Zach began his story.

As the teacher related the story to my husband and me: Zach began his story about his super-hero daddy, and when he got to the really high point of his story, his eyes lighted up and a proud grin crossed his face as he blurted out, "You know what? My Daddy can kill an elephant with a stick!" He stated the facts about his daddy's prowess with great conviction and pride, not believing for one second that he even doubted that his father could not manage such a feat.

Without a question, the best stories come from out of the mouths of babes! When I think back over the years, in many ways our son did perceive things correctly. His daddy has been a super-hero empowered by God at many times, in numerous places, and situations. He has demonstrated over and over to his son that he is a man who lifts all things up to the Lord for both his wisdom and strength. After all, isn't that what all daddy-pastors are called to do?

AN UNFORGETTABLE LUNCH

"Who gives food to all flesh, For His mercy endures forever."
Psalms 136:25

Saturday morning in our home was usually a restful time, however this one was not a typical Saturday. I was rushing to get ready so I could get over to the church, because we were hosting a Woman's Mission League spring rally for all the churches in our district. The ladies and I had worked hard on developing a good program and anticipated that it would be well-attended. As I prepared to leave the house, the children were already up watching their favorite cartoons, and my husband was working on polishing up his sermon for the week. Everything seemed in order so after saying my good-byes and giving last minute instructions to the children on cleaning their rooms, I was off.

The ladies in our church expected a good turnout on that lovely spring day, but we had an even better attendance than we had anticipated. At the end of the program the ladies chattered at the various tables where they were seated, and lunch was served along with a lovely chocolate dessert. At 1:30, the ladies in our group were cleaning up and discussing how successful the event had been with the special music group and wonderful message given by an area pastor. There was no question in our minds that our months of planning had paid off.

When I left the church, I stopped at a nearby grocery store to pick up some badly needed staples that I had been unable to get earlier in the week. With that chore accomplished and the bags of groceries in the trunk of my car, I was off for our home. Upon arriving home, I unloaded the groceries and entered the house carrying two large bags and returned to the car for the remaining two bags of groceries. Finally, my day was going to wind down, and perhaps I could sit down and relax before starting the evening meal.

By that time Zach and Annie realized I was home. They came running upstairs to tell me about their day with Dad.

They both chimed in as they said, "Mom, do you know what daddy fixed us for lunch?"

I thought to myself that it was probably something special, because my husband always enjoyed being creative with food.

I said, "No, what did your dad fix you for lunch?"

They both looked at each other and started to giggle as they blurted out, "Gizzard patty sandwiches!"

"Why gizzard patty sandwiches?" I exclaimed.

"The gizzards were all he could find that wasn't frozen, so he ground them up with the meat grinder and made patties for our sandwiches!"

I asked them how they tasted, and of course neither of them liked the gizzard patties. I laughed, and promised them if I had to go away for the day again, I'd try to have something they would like better than those gizzard patties that my husband had so creatively made on that spring Saturday when our children were still young and in the nest. However, to this day when we are all together, we often laugh as we recall that unforgettable lunch of gizzard patty sandwiches.

THE DAY BEFORE PAY DAY

"For the love of money is a root of all kinds of evil, for which some have strayed from the faith in their greediness, and pierced themselves through with many sorrows." I Tim. 6:11

As with most pastors and their young families, the day before the pay check is due the budget is often very lean. This was one of those days, and I knew I must select a thrifty cut of meat for the evening meal. Well, after some thought, I decided to go with that pound of liver I had in our freezer. I thought to myself: What better choice could one make other than to choose beef liver served with onions? A fact my mother had always told me when I was growing up was that liver and onions is a nutritious choice.

I managed to keep that in mind as I planned my inexpensive evening meal that night, although I was aware that Annie our little four-year-old, really hated liver. The rule in our home was that the children were expected to eat what was served. There was no cooking another more pleasing dish to address individual tastes. At five o'clock we sat down as a family at the dinner table and said our pre-meal blessing. With only some protests, we all ate the liver with onions, potatoes, and green beans. Annie ate the liver very slowly, but then finished it because she knew that she would then be eligible for desert after cleaning her plate.

As we finished our dinner and the thanksgiving prayer was said, I noticed that Annie was looking at me with a serious look on her face. I asked her, "What are you thinking about, Annie?" Annie's reply stunned me as she said," Mommy, I just was thinking, that I asked God to make that liver taste like steak, and it kinda did." As I chuckled to myself, I thought that the lesson I learned through this incidence was that God does answer all prayers no matter how great or how small.

THROUGH THE EYES OF A LITTLE CHILD

But Jesus said, "Let the little children come to Me, and do not forbid them; for of such is the kingdom of heaven."Matthew 19:14

The children and I were sitting in a pew two-thirds of the way back as viewed from the front of the church. This evening everyone was very quite and meditative as they reflected on the meaning of the day. It was Good Friday, the most solemn day of the church year. The day in which Jesus died on the cross as He took our place and suffered the punishment for our sins. As I sat in church meditating along with the other congregation members, I had my son on my left side and my daughter on my right side. They were just old enough to understand that we must be quiet in church and pray in order to show respect in God's house. Admittedly, these behaviors are the outward manifestations of what we hold sacred in our hearts.

As the minutes went by, I felt my little daughter tapping me on the hand to gain my attention. I dropped my head to the right in order to hear what she was so desperately trying to tell me. When I finally heard her softly spoken words she was nearly in a panic as she asked, "Mommy, why does daddy have his pants hanging on the cross?" As she finished this shocking question, I looked up only to see that my husband had carefully draped the cross with a black cloth making sure that each side was even with the other. Suddenly, I found myself giggling out loud, because through the eyes of a child, the draped cross looked exactly like those pants that my husband always seemed to hang over our dresser doors. As I thought about this scenario, I asked myself, " How would such a young child even begin to differentiate between the two?!"

IN THE DITCH

It was the last day of September, and luckily it was a bright and sunny day. It was a day in which I had much to accomplish, because our new baby was scheduled to be born on October first by caesarean section. As I thought abut the up-coming birth, I wasn't worried, because I knew the outcome was one of reward. Having a new baby in the house would give us a family with two children. My only hope was that the new one would be as wonderful as our two and half year old son had been. In my eyes, he was not only beautiful, he was also very smart.

Yes, Martin who had begun walking at nine months, kept me literally on my toes at all times. Currently, he was in the back seat of the car asking typical two-year-old questions of "What is this?", and "What is that, Mommy?" However, today my list of things was a long one in order to be ready for my ten day stay in a hospital one hundred miles away from our home.

I didn't worry about Martin because he would be well taken care of by my mother who loved him dearly. Being the first grandson, he quickly became the apple of her eye. Yes, I also remembered that my husband and I needed to run into Kansas City to pick up Grandma this evening.

As we cruised along to the grocery store, I realized that the backseat questions had ceased, and I thought to myself that perhaps he had lain down and fallen asleep. In those days, children had more freedom in the car because they were not required to be buckled up with seat belts in their car seats. However, I thought to myself that such quietness s was unusual for this time of the day, as Martin no longer took morning naps. All I needed was for him to get sick today!

As I puzzled over his quietness, I also readjusted my rearview mirror to check up on him. To my shock, there he stood stark naked in the backseat waving to all the passing cars. I literally lost control of the car as I tried to reach in that backseat to get him to sit down. Yes, naked Martin and his very pregnant mommy ended up in the ditch. I'm not sure who was more upset, he or me? However, the incident did get the attention of many gapers, and the help of a tow truck soon came to rescue naked Martin and big old me!

I now muse and think what a lasting impression we must have given in that small Missouri town where my husband was the only pastor for miles around. I now ask myself, how is it that some PK's (preacher kids) seem to gain a reputation for being overly precocious children; even the ones that cause their mothers to drive into the ditch?

"Children's children are the crown of old men, and the glory of children is their father." Proverbs 17:6

10

PETS IN THE PARSONAGE

"A dog teachers a boy fidelity, perseverance, and how to turn around three times before lying down."

-Robert Benchly"

ODE TO ALI

" . . .And God made the beast of the earth according to its kind...
Then God saw everything that He had made, and indeed it was
very good. . . . Then the Lord God took the man and put him in the
garden of Eden to tend and keep it.. . . And the Lord God said,
"It is not good that man should be alone; I will make him a helper
comparable to him." Out of the ground the Lord God formed
every beast of the field and every bird of the air, and brought them
to Adam to see what he would call them. " (Genesis 1 and 2)

My husband feels that when it comes to me and animals, we are still in the "Garden of Eden": every beast and bird seems to find their way to our house. It is true that I (Eve) have taken over for Adam and take my job very seriously. I have shared that mission with our children as well. Over the years we have enjoyed:

Cats and bats and big white rats
Dogs and frogs and polly wogs
Gerbils, hamsters, guinea pigs,
Fish and turtles, small and big
Raccoons, squirrels and curly sheep
Crickets, lizards, birds that peep

Spiders, geese, and hens that cluck
Horses, turkeys, big white ducks
Mice and crabs and one thing more
Snakes that glide across the floor!

This is the story of Ali, the alley cat. Ali found his way to our animal "sanctuary" one summer day shortly after our Siamese cat had presented us with a litter of kittens. He also appeared to be a pure Siamese that had been on his own for awhile. He was thin, disheveled, had a piece missing from his ear, and looked as though he had been abused He was weary of people but obviously in need of help. When I went to pick him up, he bit me. (The only animal, wild or otherwise, that has ever done this.) This earned him room and board in a cozy cage for six weeks until it was certain that he did not have rabies. He looked like he was a fighter (necessary for him to have survived on his own and in the wild), so I named him Mohammed Ali. Ali for short.

Ali reveled in the gentle attention, care, and food given to him by me and the children. In time he plumped out into a beautiful, loving cat. He kept himself well groomed, he purred, and got a lot of well needed rest. His confinement period over, he was released to explore his new home. He discovered our female and kittens in no time flat and immediately got into the box with them. "Oh no! " I cried, rushing to save the kittens.

Male cats will often kill kittens that are not their own and sometimes those that are. Both Ali and Peanuts (the mother) looked up at me quizzically with their piercing blue eyes as if to say, "What's the problem?" ; then Ali returned to what he was doing, licking the kittens, not killing them! Later when I took Ali to the vet for shots and neutering, I discussed the odd behavior to the vet. He informed me that Siamese cats are different from most cats. Besides their blue eyes and "cougar belly", Siamese cats are extremely intelligent; and the males help to take care of kittens, whether theirs or not. In the days that followed, one of the kittens who was later named Tigger, was particularly found of "dad" and followed him everywhere. They became constant companions for many years.

However, Ali had a problem. Although he was very loving to his cat family, the children, and me; he did not trust anyone else. This became evident when he would not let my husband touch him. In fact, Ali soon learned Ed's schedule and would wait on the chair by the door when it was time for him to come home from church; whereupon, he would leap off the chair and bite him in the leg. Ali was protecting " his domain". Ed would throw him out into the snow to teach him who was the "alpha cat", and I would later let Ali in when both males had "cooled" off. The rest of the evening they would sit in their respective corners glaring at one another until the scene would repeat itself the next day.

This all changed one day, when my husband was lying on the couch watching TV and eating a ham sandwich. Lured by the smell of meat, Ali, slowly approached the source. I watched from a distance as my husband slowly offered him a piece of meat, and then another, and then another. I held my breath as Ali leaped onto his chest for the final piece. That finished, he washed his face and paws and curled up for a nap on my husband's chest. Six months of "war" ended that night with a simple peace offering. There is a lesson to be learned there. In the years that followed, Ali often liked to "groom" my husband, only growling at him if he didn't sit still until he was finished

But all of Ali's demons had not yet been conquered. Ali was an attack cat in every sense of the word. He protected his family, us, from the outside world. He would not let anyone else enter the house without attacking them. If we had guests, we had to lock Ali in the basement. Then the day came when my husband accepted a new call and we would move from Missouri to Ohio. However, we were not able to move into our new home until the sellers had a chance to vacate: six weeks into the school year. Since I had a new teaching position to report to, this necessitated my driving the old pickup and tent camper to Ohio with our children while my husband stayed behind to finish up his job and make arrangements for moving the contents of our home.

It was a happy day when Ed and the pets arrived in Ohio, and we were finally able to move from tent to house. As we waited for the movers to arrive, the pets busily sniffed out their new abode. I ran to the door at the anticipated knock. There stood two burly men each at least six feet tall. I greeted them with a happy smile and said, "Bring it on in! We have been waiting for you!" They were not smiling.

"Where's your cat?" they asked.

"Which one?" I curiously replied.

"The attack cat!"

"Oh, Ali. He is locked on the patio."

"That's what your husband said at the other house. The cat opens doors. We are not coming in until we are assured the cat is contained!"

Apparently, Ed forgot that Ali could open doors, and in his haste had put Ali in our bedroom instead of the basement. It would appear that in an alter**CAT**ion between a seven pound cat and two burly six foot moving men, Ali had won. "Hail to the champion!" We certainly did not want our cat to offend or hurt anyone, but the picture of one little cat winning against two burly men seemed awfully funny. I must interject here that Ali went for the legs, and if people had on long pants, they were well protected from Ali's claws. Nevertheless, a mad cat protecting his territory is not something to take lightly. I assured the men that Ali was locked on the patio and had not yet had enough time to figure out how to open sliding doors. Assured of their safety, the men quickly unloaded our furniture. However, I couldn't help but notice their frequent furtive looks in the direction of the patio. They were not happy men.

We hoped in time that Ali would learn to trust other people as well as ourselves; however, when animals have been abused, they sometimes never learn to trust anyone ever again. Some, unfortunately, have to be put down. Ali, fortunately, learned to trust other people as long as they didn't attempt to touch him. If they approached him, he would give that low growl warning them to stay away. Siamese don't bother with hissing and spitting and slapping.

They growl. Ignore the growl, and they won't scratch but bite. They are all business. Everyone we knew, knew Ali, and knew to admire him at a distance. He had undoubtedly had a very hard life, but he had learned to overcome most of it. He was a magnifiCAT, loving animal to those he trusted. But Ali had another secret that surprised us all.

We lived next door to a blueberry farm. Each year in July, our elderly neighbors converted their three car garage into a store for blueberry pickers and the sale of produce. For the next two months, there was the excitement of people and cars and Amish buggies arriving early in the morning and until dark to pick and buy berries. One day, I went over to talk to Betty about something and was shocked to see Ali, toes tucked under in a relaxed position, sitting on their cash register as though this was his rightful place in life. I quickly apologized and went to retrieve my cat. Everyone knew that "Ali bites!" But Betty stopped me. I learned that Ali had been coming there every day since blueberry season started. He liked to sit on the register and watch the people. Ali liked people!

"But he bites," I said. "We could all be sued! And Ali put down!"

" No problem," she said, and pointed to a sign next to the register. It read. "Do not touch the register. The cat bites!" Obviously, Ali had formed a business relationship with Betty!

God created the animals and then people to care for them. Sometimes people unfortunately forget that. As for me and my family, we never cease to be amazed at all of God's creation, and are thankful for all the furry, feathered, scaley things that share our world, our hearts, our homes, and sometimes (if we are lucky or not so lucky) our beds!

THE LIFE OF "SOME SQUIRREL"

"Any calls this morning?" I asked entering the office after a morning check of the halls. I was the principal of a Lutheran School.

"Just one," the secretary replied. "A lady called about an abandoned baby squirrel and wondered if someone at the school could come get it."

"Well, that's different," I responded, wondering what had possessed her to call a school.

"I can't go right now because I have a class to teach, but if you have her address, I will check it out in an hour." Apparently our school mission was extended to include helpless animals.

At that point, our custodian who had entered the office with me volunteered for "rescue duty", and an hour later I peered into a makeshift nest of envelope box with cotton carefully arranged by our secretary. A hairless little creature with eyes sealed shut lay very still. Further investigation revealed that he was at least physically unhurt that I could see but was covered with fleas! Two days alone on the ground without any food, it was a wonder he was still alive. What a way to enter the world! With a carton of milk from the cafeteria and an eye dropper from the science lab, I fed "our little guest" his first meal. At home that night, I continued to feed him on an hourly basis, and life seemed to slowly ebb into his little body.

Before retiring for the evening, I placed his "nest" in an empty bird cage for the night.

At 3:00 a.m. our household was awakened by the loudest, most shrill noise I have ever heard. Lights flipped on, and I searched the house for the source of the ruckus. Who would believe that this tiny, near death little creature could make such a siren of a sound!

"What's wrong with it?" my sleepy husband asked rubbing his eyes.

"I think he's hungry. Go back to bed. I'll feed him." Like any newborn, for the next week, his siren like squeak woke me at 3:00 a.m. for a feeding. Gradually he began to sleep through the night (thank goodness), but he had earned his name: Squeak!

Since Squeak needed to be fed often on a regular basis, he accompanied me to school each day where either I or the school secretary would feed him hourly. After several weeks, his eyes opened and I could see why perhaps his mother had pushed him out of the nest. Squeak was born with just one eye. He would never survive in the wild because of a lack of peripheral vision. He became a permanent member of our family.

Soon little teeth began to emerge. He still couldn't chew acorns or nuts, so I began to try other foods to see what he liked: cookies, crackers, and some fruits, as I remember. In time he advanced to nuts and acorns. He preferred walnuts and pecans and cashews, but would not eat peanuts unless they were M&M's , and no, the chocolate candy covering never hurt him!

Hair began growing on his tail so that it became obvious that he was indeed a squirrel and not a rat. He would sit on my shoulder while I took him into various classrooms where the students could learn and see firsthand how a squirrel develops. They would gather acorns and bring them to school and watch him gradually develop into a beautiful fox squirrel.

Squeak liked to curl up in the sleeve of my sweater while I graded papers or watched T.V., but as he got older, he refused to go to bed in his cage. When I tried to extract him from my sweater sleeve, it became a wrestling match. Finally, the only way I could get the "squirrely" creature out of my sweater was to go to bed with sweater and squirrel still on. Gradually, as he settled down and went to sleep, I was able to carefully, slowly, remove the sleeping Squeak and put him in his own bed.

In time, he outgrew his bird cage. I then designed a new home that my husband built just for Squeak. I wanted it to be as much as a natural habitat for him as possible, and I didn't want him to feel isolated or lonely. The cage was six feet high, eight feet wide, and four feet deep. It was painted flat black and covered with rabbit wire. Inside were several perches at different levels and angles, a nesting box, and a long hollow log that my husband had found. Since we couldn't afford a china closet anyway, we placed Squeak's cage in a central location in the dining room where he could see everyone coming into the house and me preparing meals in the kitchen. Upon seeing the cage, visitors expected something large like a gibbon ape or a dozen macaws, and were always surprised that it housed just one little squirrel.

I began to be concerned about how Squeak would learn to be a squirrel and if it would just come naturally. I would soon have my answer. At times, Squeak was permitted the run of the house even though we had a large dog and two cats. We began to find nuts hidden in shoes, under cushions, in coat pockets, and germinating in my flower pots. Once I observed him carefully placing a nut under our sleeping dog and patting it down as if in soil. It was obvious that Squeak was storing food for winter. God had supplied him with all the instincts that he would need to live as a squirrel even without a squirrel family to teach him!

Squeak also knew he had to chew things to keep his teeth from growing too big in his mouth. Squeak knew this but we did not until we began to find chew marks on anything wooden- like furniture, pianos, etc. Once while I was reading next to a lamp, the light suddenly went out and I heard a sharp "squeak!". Squeak had mistakenly chewed the electric wire and gotten shocked! Fortunately he was O.K., and my husband knew to supply appropriate chewing logs in his cage from that point on.

Squeak became a regular member of our family. During the summer, Squeak's cage was placed on our screened in porch, and he was allowed to roam free when it was not in use. I, my husband, son, and daughter took turns holding him and playing with him so that he didn't get lonely. A favorite game of his was chasing my daughter's brightly painted toenails as if they were some sort of new nut delicacy! We searched for months for a stuffed life-like toy squirrel for him to play with. When my husband finally found one, Squeak was in heaven playing with his new companion.

Then one day it happened. Squeak grew up. It was obvious that he was an alpha male and would not tolerate any other males in his domain. My husband and son could no longer hold him. In fact, Squeak had to be kept in his cage whenever there were males in the house. Even so, when guests visited, females could approach his cage with no problem. If a male walked into the house, Squeak would charge at them, chattering his teeth. I don't know how he could distinguish males from females but it definitely wasn't by the clothes they wore. If he happened to be out of his cage, he would chase and bite them - another instinct kicking in! However this instinct would one day save his life.

I was walking in the backyard with Squeak on my shoulder. He was allowed to run in the grass and climb trees, always coming to my call. One day he was playing in the grass when I noticed our neighbor's three cats come toward us and begin to form a circle around our squirrel. With his lack of peripheral vision, Squeak couldn't see what was happening and for the first time, he didn't come when I called. He wasn't finished with "what he was doing". Desperate to get him out of harm's way, I did the only thing I knew to do. I called for my son. George came running and saw what was happening. I told him to prop the door open, call "Squeak", and be prepared to run!

"SQUEAK!" he called.

Squeak looked up from what he was doing and turned that one good eye in the direction of the sound. Seeing George, he took off and the chase was on! Through the patio, the family room, the dining room, the living room, and onto George's bedroom. Squeak was right on his heals when George ran into his room and slammed the door as quickly as possible. "Smack!" was the sound as Squeak hit the door. Chattering in anger and indignation, I carefully replaced him in his habitat for a cooling off spell. Little did he know that another male had just saved his life!

Squirrels in the wild live on an average of seven years. Squeak lived to be twelve years old, and then one winter he developed a cough and eventually stopped eating. He died shortly after. I believe he had succumbed to heart disease. He was mourned as we do when we lose any loved one. I believe that Squeak lived a full and happy life if somewhat different from other squirrels

Life with Squeak was an education as well as an adventure. We learned to decipher the meanings in tail flicks, front paw positions, behavior, and vocal sounds. We marveled at the instincts that God places in His creatures. Parenting in the parsonage, in our case at least, has always gone hand in hand with pets in the parsonage, be they domesticated or wild , sharing our lives with other animals has always been a trust and a calling. Not many can say that they have been kissed by a squirrel, but Squeak shared his kisses with me and my family, and it was a blessing that I will forever cherish.

"And God made the beast of the earth according to its kind, cattle according to its kind, and everything that creeps on the earth according to its kind. And God saw that it was good." (Genesis 1: 25)

A LASTING IMPRESSION

After another long autumn day at the office, my husband finally had some time to relax and even find time to play with the children. He took Zach and Annie outside along with Cocoa, our chocolate poodle. Cocoa had instantly become a family member after we purchased him for the children. He loved to play and romp with the children whenever he had the opportunity. The only rule was that he be kept close by at all times, because Cocoa loved to run off and visit other folks in our neighborhood.

This evening as the sun was setting my husband spotted the new neighbor lady who just moved in the house facing our back yard. Being a cordial person, he walked over with Cocoa leading on his leash. As I stood washing the dishes from the evening meal, and peering out of the window, I noted that the neighbor also had her dog on a leash. Her dog was a cute little Shiatsu with long flowing hair. As I watched the encounter, I noted how well the dogs also seemed to meet each other.

As my husband welcomed our new neighbor and extended his hand to shake hers, to my horror, I saw our precious Cocoa gently lift his left hind leg and urinate on our new neighbor's sweet little Shiatsu. Suddenly my husband glanced down only to discover what was taking place, and I immediately saw his neck and face turn beet-red. To this day we remember how embarrassed we both were; however , Cocoa took the incident in his stride, as he proudly trotted home probably thinking that he had welcomed his new friend with the best doggie manners he knew. There is no doubt in our minds that he indeed did leave a lasting impression!

"A man who flatters his neighbor spreads a net for his feet."
Proverbs 29:5

11

HAPPY ENDINGS

"There is danger in probing the future with too short a stick. Excellence takes time."

- Edgar Dale

WHAT NOW, O LORD ?

*"Your ears shall hear a word behind you, saying, This is the way,
walk in it, Whenever you turn to the right hand Or whenever you
turn to the left." Isaiah 30:21*

As usual I was in a hurry to get to class. After bravely driving in
the hectic Chicago morning traffic, it was always a relief to get to
school safely and to also get a parking place. This morning was
no different from most others. To my delight I bumped into my
graduate advisor in the hallway as I approached my early class.
She always was pleasant, but this morning she asked me if I would
consider being her graduate assistant. What an opportunity for me!
The time was right, my children were out of the nest; my son was the
proud father of two wonderful sons, and my daughter was traveling
nationally and internationally sharing her talents through her call to
musical ministry. However, I knew that I now needed a new direction
in which I could be used. So after much prayerful consideration, off
to school I went. I had turned to God many times and asked, What
now oh Lord? Yes, He was answering my questions and giving me
a new direction for my life. With this new opportunity to serve as a
graduate assistant, I could really experience higher education at its
fullest: planning, teaching, and studying, studying. . . . .

However, with the opportunity to serve as my advisor's teaching assistant, I also discovered that I really loved working and teaching in higher education, and was able to give back to my current students what I had gained in experience through my own teaching profession. As time went by, God opened doors and windows for me, and there was no question in my mind that I should pursue a Ph.D. So, off to Dr. School I went while teaching full-time at another university. My life was inundated with attending meetings, advising students, grading papers, attending more meetings, more advising, more teaching, and yes, more planning. This all was part of my work life, but additionally I also was diligently studying, researching, and writing in order to gain a Ph.D.

I now ask myself, how did I do all of that? It was not easy, even though my husband was very supportive and cooked many meals during that phase in our lives. I worked almost around the clock on many days, studying for classes, then studying for my comps, doing my dissertation and the research that it involved, and finally after nearly five years the dissertation defense. Yes, I had lived through it, and could look forward to graduation day.

Now with a Ph.D., I am beginning to think about the next phase in my life, and once again asking God to show me the way. It is true, life has taught me that He will lead me in the direction he wants me to go. And, perhaps it will be a time to just play with my dog, talk to my dear husband, perhaps have another grandchild??, study my Bible, or just smell the roses.

Now I'm ready for the next chapter to unfold. Ready set, here I come! After all, when God is for you, who can be against you? There's no question, my blessings have been numerous, and my cup has overflowed! On God's path, I have been led into areas of life I would never have dreamed of delving into, and now I'm looking forward to a new direction from Him.

GOD'S A "MAZE" ING CALLING

Elementary school is over so quickly, and the next thing you know you are in Junior High School, and some advisor is asking you what you want to be/do when you grow up. You are thirteen years old and are faced with the decision that may determine the rest of your life! You are told that you must make a decision in order that the advisor may sign you up for the right courses to start you on your way. My choices were: college prep, secretarial, agriculture, general education, or special education.

In first grade, I had wanted to be a trapeze artist. It's a good thing I had changed my mind by seventh grade, because they didn't have a category for aerialists. By seventh grade, I had decided to become a minister. You can imagine my disappointment when my Lutheran School teacher told me that it was impossible for me to become a minister. Only men could become ministers. He recommended that I become a teacher. The die was cast!

Time went by, and I eventually married another teacher I had met in college. More time went by, and he eventually became a minister making me a minister's wife. That's when life became really interesting. My role often was to do what needed to be done that no one else was doing or wanted to do or ever thought to do. It became a wonderful outlet for creative endeavors and an opportunity to experience new things. Some of the things that one might expect were to teach Sunday School, Vacation Bible School, camp, and adult Bible classes. Then came using puppetry, sacred storytelling, and the liturgical clown for the children's talk in church, and organizing the church picnic. Making church banners, leading choir, and playing the organ or accordion came later..

I helped with the gardening and trimmed hedges around the church, started a preschool, started and taught in a senior center, and painted a mural on the back wall of the fellowship hall. Creative money makers, dinners, and fellowship activities were always in demand. Then my realm began to expand. I started writing Christian curriculum and devotional materials for Concordia Publishing House. A call was extended to serve in the mission field in Czech Republic for four months. I was trained as an Ambassador of Reconciliation for my church district, and was sent as a lay representative to the synodical theological conference.

Lest this sound like a list of "How Great I Am", nothing could be further from the truth. I was given the opportunity to share and learn through these activities. It is rather, "How Great God Is", that even someone such as I with limited abilities could be given the opportunity to experience the richness of God's ministry. Some things I did well, and others, not so well; but the opportunity and effort were there nevertheless. Then something unusual happened.

I decided on going back to college to get an advanced degree. Since my chosen minor was in counseling, I was taking a course on "Career Counseling" . Unlike when I was in junior high and high school, they now have electronic programs where students answer a variety of questions. Based on their answers, three careers are then recommended for the student. Each of the twenty teachers in my college class was invited to become familiar with the equipment. We laughed at the thought that we would discover that we had chosen the wrong profession. Each student took a turn and was pleased to learn that they had chosen the right profession and were also given two alternatives that they might have also chosen. I was the last person to try out the program.

Students gathered around to see my results. Of twenty teachers, I was the only one that apparently had chosen the wrong profession. Additionally, it only recommended one choice: not three. The recommendation was: MINISTER. I went home saddened by the thought that I never got to fulfill "my dream". At least, the program thought I should be a minister. The machine didn't know I was a woman.

Flash forward about twenty years to the present. The other day, an elderly member of our congregation paid me a compliment I couldn't believe. She said, " you are the best minister's wife we have ever had. You are always there for us, no matter what the need." I was stunned by her compliment. True I have tried to fill in where needed. I give it my best try, but sometimes that is all it is - a try (like playing the organ when I don't know anything about it. I just turn it on and play the keys: sometimes without mistakes.)

My life has been a maze going down one path after another: sometimes hitting a dead end, but progressing toward the goal nevertheless. I can't quite see the end to my maze yet, but I have traveled at least three-fourths of the way. I don't know if it will be a straight "shot" from now on or if there will be yet a few more turns in my travel before I reach my end. In reflection, I have finally seen how God has led me where He wanted me to be and to my initial career choice after all.

I, personally, am glad that I am not an ordained minister. I would not care for all of the responsibilities an ordained minister has. Instead, I have enjoyed the variety, challenges, and opportunity for creativity and learning that I have been blessed to experience. I am convinced: that God calls BOTH men and women to ministry, and ministry can take many forms, especially when we least expect it.

"And we know that all things work together for good to those who love God, to those who are the called according to His purpose."
(Rom. 8:28)

HAPPY ENDING!

QUESTIONS FOR REFLECTION/DISCUSSION

CHAPTER 1 ▬▬▬▬▬▬▬▬▬▬▬▬▬▬▬▬▬▬▬▬▬▬▬▬▬

- Have you ever felt that God has led you to a particular spot or situation?
- How do you know when God is giving you a direction in your decision making for major life decisions?
- In what ways have you knowingly responded to God's call?

CHAPTER 2 ▬▬▬▬▬▬▬▬▬▬▬▬▬▬▬▬▬▬▬▬▬▬▬▬▬

- How does God speak to you through nature?
- Has God ever reassured you of His presence through things experienced in nature? Talk about it. CHAPTER 3.
- How have relationships within your family or outside of your family helped you to better understand God?
- Are you able to see God in others?

CHAPTER 4 ▬▬▬▬▬▬▬▬▬▬▬▬▬▬▬▬▬▬▬▬▬▬▬▬▬

- What are some things that you never thought you'd do in life, but nonetheless have achieved?
- Have you been able to see in retrospect, how God has been directing your life's circumstances?

CHAPTER 5 ▬▬▬▬▬▬▬▬▬▬▬▬▬▬▬▬▬▬▬▬

- Do you feel that God allows you to have trials and tribulations in your life? If so why?
- Sometimes it is difficult to see the good that might come from certain circumstances. Have you ever faced such struggles?
- How do you handle situations that "go wrong"?
- What advice might you give to others in a similar situation?
- In what ways might your faith have grown through the various trials that you've experienced?

CHAPTER 6 ▬▬▬▬▬▬▬▬▬▬▬▬▬▬▬▬▬▬▬▬

- What is the biggest mountain-top experience that you've had during your life-time?
- When were you "in a valley"?
- What helped you to get out of "the valley"?

CHAPTER 7 ▬▬▬▬▬▬▬▬▬▬▬▬▬▬▬▬▬▬▬▬

- What is your church's current style of ministry?
- Do you feel that God calls and equips different individuals to serve in different types of churches?
- What are some of the memorable experiences you've experienced within your church?

CHAPTER 8 ▬▬▬▬▬▬▬▬▬▬▬▬▬▬▬▬▬▬▬▬

- How does the community in which you live effect the life-style of the members in your church?
- How is a church like a family?

CHAPTER 9 ▬▬▬▬▬▬▬▬▬▬▬▬▬▬▬▬▬▬▬▬

- What do you see are the greatest challenges to parenting these days?
- What advice would you give to parents?
- It has become commonplace, even necessary, in many

families today for both parents to work outside of the home. What are some of the challenges that face these families today and what advice might you have for newly weds facing this choice?

- What are the biggest blessings that you have experienced as a parent in raising children in the parsonage?
- What are the biggest deterrents that you have experiences as a parent in raising children in the parsonage?
- How have your children responded or been affected by being raising in the parsonage setting?

CHAPTER 10

- If you have pets, how have they been a blessing to you?
- Pets have been proven to be very beneficial and therapeutic to people. Talk about a special pet or pet relationship in your life.
- In what ways can we carry out the task given to Adam and Eve in the garden to care for God's creatures?

CHAPTER 11

- Over the years that you and your family have served God, what are some instances that you can recall that have had happy endings?
- When you were little, what did you want to be when you grew up? How has that dream been fulfilled?
- At what point do you see yourself in your life's journey? Are there some things that you would like to try or do in the time that you have left?

Printed in the United States
146706LV00001B/1/P